Profits,
Power
& Piety

Profits, Power & Piety

by
JAMES L. JOHNSON
Author of: *A Handful of Dominoes, The Nine Lives of Alphonse, A Piece of the Moon Is Missing, What Every Woman Should Know About a Man, Before Honor* and *Code Name Sabastion*

HARVEST HOUSE PUBLISHERS
Irvine, California 92714

ACKNOWLEDGMENTS

Material from *Corporation Man* by Antony Jay. © 1971 by International Handelsmaatschappij Cypres NV, used by permission of Random House, Inc., New York, N.Y.

Material from *The Effective Executive* by Peter F. Drucker, © 1967, used by permission of Harper & Row, Publishers, New York, N.Y.

Material from *Psychoanalysis and Religion*, © 1950 by Erich Fromm. Bantam Books edition, used by permission of Yale University Press, New Haven, Conn.

To Kenneth N. Taylor whose leadership and counsel have helped immeasurably in encouraging toward the honesty and candor reflected in this book.

Simon's Signposts to Glory Inc. and Alexander Simon have no basis in fact as being an actual organization or a person and are, therefore, not intended to reflect any one group or individual. Both are used as the extreme case in point and serve as a model to illustrate the *real* problems and syndromes that may, and in some cases *do*, dominate the business-ministry when allowed to go unchecked. Case histories are drawn from actual experiences and are so identified.

PROFITS, POWER AND PIETY

(Previously published as The Nine-to-Five Complex, ©1972 by the Zondervan Corporation.)

Copyright ©1980 Harvest House Publishers
Irvine, California 92714

Library of Congress Catalog Card Number: 72-83881
ISBN 0-89081-2403

All rights reserved. No portion of this book may be used in any form without the written permission of the publisher.

Printed in the United States of America.

In dedication to
the Alexander Simons
who can yet be
God's heroes
in history
who keep on believing
and to the
Nine-to-Five Warriors

Contents

Introduction 9

Who Is Alexander Simon? 17

The Ministry 19

The Business 20

Chapter 1   The Nine-to-Five Complex 21

Chapter 2   The Problem 39

Chapter 3   The Organization — The Incredible Journey 54

Chapter 4   The Group — I Only Work Here? ... 80

Chapter 5   The Status Complex — Up the Down Staircase? 103

Chapter 6   The Law and Order Complex — We Like Sheep? 128

Chapter 7   Will Success Spoil Alexander Simon? .155

The Prayer of the Nine-to-Five Warrior 177

The Prayer of the Leader 178

INTRODUCTION

Perhaps no era in church history has been so distinctly marked by a sense of Christian industrial enterprise as that beginning at the end of World War II to the present. If the early and middle nineteen-hundreds were characterized by unprecedented missionary zeal and movement, certainly the last thirty years must go into the record as the "hour of the CNP" (Church National Product).

Not that this has been so terribly bad, at least on the surface. Books, key chains, tee-shirts advertising Jesus as The Way, Satan kits, bumper stickers, and "born again certificates by mail" surely play some part in the bent of contemporary church history. Insurance package deals have made protection a lot easier for the saints in their sunset years; consultant teams on everything on "how to invest the Lord's dollar and still take it with you" to "getting the biggest bang out of the buck in tax breaks" have undoubtedly altered the course of the pilgrim journey considerably. Or who can deny the immeasurable returns on the exotic Bible cruises into the Caribbean on the first class luxury liner?

Still, one has to view this record production as a kind of "sanctified hustling" and, therefore, with some mixed emotions. While there is some pride in the Christian in knowing he is not far behind his secular peer in terms of goods and services, there is nevertheless an uncertain sound of brass clanging in the temple. God's gold is being counterfeited, and this certain or uncertain awareness is what is eating at the vitals of what could be or should be a much more spiritually charged church. It is certainly true in light of all this that there can hardly be any credence for that word of the Lord, "The children of mammon are wiser than the children of light." (Luke 16:13) But in accomplishing that hurdle, something has been lost at the same time, much more than the Lord ever intended.

Again, granted that all this flurry of manufacturing in the name of the Lord is based on good intentions for the most part, there is at the same time a rightful uneasiness creeping into the "inner circle" of the money changers. The emergence of the contradiction evident in "profits, power, and piety" smarts the conscience of any manufacturer, salesman or corporation director, provided, of course, that the conscience has not already been seared to numbness. It is difficult, if not totally impossible, to detach oneself from the image of Christ in the Gospels who had no place to lay His head to the velvet lined palaces that most successful Christian corporation heads now own. One senses a taint of secularism coming in with the hawking voices of the Christian salesman in the marketplace, tooting his horns, and bouncing his balloons in an attempt to draw the wary saint who is not wholly convinced as yet that he or she should traffic in these holy images.

And yet, apart from the image the world gets of this odd charade in the name of God, and even apart from all the diverse products, the real concern in the end comes down to the people behind it. There are all kinds of hero types in church history who had a clear path to martyrdom and pursued it in full awareness of its final implications. These were the fortunate ones. There also are the named and nameless who struggled in their personal Gethsemanes, sweating blood to hold down their corner of the Shekinah Glory; these, likewise, knew something of Cause.

But the man or woman caught in the Christian industrial complex is totally rare in this regard. The worker. No one struggles more with the contradictions of "profits, power, and piety" than the people inside these manufacturing plants. These must "die daily" to the peculiar mix of profits with ministry. Their death is seldom, if ever, noticed. These won't make the roll call in glory for shutting the mouths of lions or quenching the violence of fire or waxing valiant in fight; all they will earn perhaps is a footnote that says they simply endured, and only God Himself knows what that has meant in its fullest dimension.

It is this *Christian organization man* that this book is all about. It is about that "nine-to-five" warrior who has committed himself or herself to some sense of contribution to the Kingdom but who suffers daily the contradictions of the ministry-business or vice versa. They are "small" people in the hierarchy of Christian bureaucracy, the typists, the secretaries, the shipping room clerks, the bookkeepers.

This book is not about the countless victories they have experienced, for quite honestly many of them are not really sure of the nature of the battle they are in; it is not about their trophies in converts, because few, if any, of them have any idea of how shorthand, balance sheets, waxed floors, clean washrooms, or the inventory of paper clips actually contribute to the ultimate goal of evangelism or church growth.

Again, this book is not about their victorious prayer life, because what they pray about mostly—order, structure, goals, values, purpose, sense of direction, motivation, and leadership—are not the usual list of prayer requests. So they remain like the Jews in a committee meeting at the foot of the Red Sea, committed to launch, but with no boats and, as in the case of the organization man too often, no Moses in sight.

This is not even about their sense of "blessed oneness" or the "unity of the faith" that goes with a sense of glorious teamwork someone told them about once when they were first hired. Most of them know only the grim realities of isolation and alienation and the necessity of operating behind enclosed department partitions that serve more as watertight doors against the flood of organizational chaos rising around them.

This book is not about the glorious sense of "full-time Christian work" because the "nine-to-five" knows only overtime without remuneration in most instances.

It is not even about the rewards of dedication, because their world is too often summed up in terms of "if you succeed it is by the grace of God; if you fail it is your fault."

What all this says is that the Christian organization man caught in the "profits, power, and piety" syndrome has his price to pay, far more perhaps than his secular peer. The "cost of discipleship" for him is immense.

What this book is *about* too is that, despite all of this, the Christian organization man hangs in there when so many others quit. The question posed in this book, among others, is: what holds him or her?

Again, this book is about this real "third world" of Christian service that so few in the church understand or even recognize as legitimate Christian service. For even though the Christian "nine-to-fiver" is a missionary in the truest sense, he is never accepted as such, because any man or woman who works the vineyard for money—daily bread really—has forfeited the right to be named among those who "sacrifice." And this book is about this man or woman who cannot fit the image of a "legitimate business professional" either, for "after all, everybody knows he's in Christian industry because he or she couldn't make it in the real world of secular business with its heat of competition."

Beyond this, of course, and even more significantly perhaps, this book is about the Christian "nine-to-fiver's" peculiar life style that goes with the Christian organization man caught in the world of "profit, power, and piety." It is a profile of tragicomedies at times that comes so often in direct relation to his work environment. It is an attempt to analyze that environment. It is an attempt to dissect the ingredients that account for so much of the confusion, disorganization, loss of morale, and what one has called "the problems of a negotiable peace with myself and others."

What's more, this book is an attempt to focus as well on the keeper of this vineyard, the theocratic ruler, founder, controller, and master of the household who must, ultimately, stand or fall before God on the stewardship entrusted to him—namely people, not products. But who, for all of his failures and sometimes his own confusion in trying to bring "profits, power, and piety" together into some kind of synchrony, is not totally without awareness that all is not well in the "Good Ship Grace."

This book likewise constitutes the writer's concerns as reflected in a study of Christian organizations over a period of three years, those ranging from "non-profit" to "profit" with more attention on the latter. This book is *not* a book on management as such. I leave that to the experts. But it does encompass the basic principles of business management which, if applied, could go a long way to alleviating the frustration, futility, and often total lack of morale within the Christian organization. The book is not intended to be a caustic commentary on the contradictions of the Kingdom being run on money or being used to get money. There is humor and certainly tragicomedy. But such is the truth of the matter. All of it, hopefully, will help somewhat to bring awareness of the broken fences and the torn-down hedges of people's lives and, if allowed to remain, can only bring irreparable damage to the cause and the name of God. Hopefully it will gain the attention of those who have the responsibility and authority so that they will see the need for correction, redesign, and some rethinking.

The ultimate purpose of the book is to bring attention to the fact that the Christian organization must always be one step higher than its secular peer in terms of motivation and certainly in terms of the custodialship of people. Since the writing of this book in 1972 when it appeared in hardcover (Zondervan Publishing Co.), more than 300 new organizations and profit groups have emerged under the umbrella of the church. Churches themselves are emerging as corporations, with business managers, business offices, products (cassettes, etc.). All of this may be fine and in order, but if God's people in them are damaged or mutilated by "kingdom building," God's judgement in the end has to fall.

Finally, this book written in this vein is done so only because there is a sense of optimism, cautious as it may be, within the Christian organization rank and file who believe that Christian leadership is not totally inured to the grievances that have accumulated. There is a tremendous wealth of positive energy within Christian work today that, if properly harnessed and motivated, could bring a spiritual impact that could be felt in world-wide dimensions. And it is a good sign to note that the leadership, at least in some areas, is gradually coming to realize this and is making some kind of move to effect a change.

If the sharing of this material does nothing more than focus on this peculiar "profits, power, and piety" syndrome, with its intrinsic dangers, and then bring new awareness in terms of what God must be suffering in it, that is enough. If this book will help some president, owner, director, chairman, or whatever leadership designation is involved, to likewise become aware of the silent cry beyond the clank and roar of the machinery, then it will have been worth the hours of research, preparation, and the writing.

There is a principle of service and labor that is peculiarly characteristic of the kingdom of God. If we have missed it along the way, this in itself does not spell disaster. But to know we have missed it and not search for it and use it—this finally is the road to judgement.

Hopefully this book might become some kind of roadblock on the one hand, but on the other I trust it will become a signpost to better things.

—J.L. Johnson

Who Is Alexander Simon?

He is — or was — of course, myself. No one else perhaps? Perhaps. I do not seek to attribute my own failures to others. But I do know the fear of what even the smallest grain of wrong can do in the vineyard when allowed to grow as weed. In 1965-66 I saw myself as I was — "Simon." There was some good even then in me, in what God had given from the beginning of His love — but something else had been added, which I sensed was not of Him, that would, if nursed, destroy me in the end. For that one who kindly in the Lord revealed that I was dispensing more misery than light, I am forever grateful.

And yet I have not yet fully arrived, as those around me and under me, know well, even though my "Simon" is in the past. I fight him every day, for he would again lay hold of me if he could, that side of him, I mean, that gave no light and bred the growth of lesser things and even crippling spirit.

So if perchance there be a "Simon" even as I was, take heart. I have lived to say, "It need not be." I know your domain may be larger than my own and more complex. More difficult to change? Perhaps. But God works the same to help us come to terms, to rise to what He wants us to be. For there are those, as there were for me, who hold you close as precious to themselves and God. They want to help!

So this is the great mystery of the Kingdom! That those who may hurt because of my poor command and uncertain course I take are yet the first to rush to my side in my struggle with God to attain! Trust them to do you well! But first, as I, do your thing! As small as it may be or large, confess your humanity and loss. And then take the resources to learn and build anew! And then find the riches of His grace — for you and them! And then know at last, SUCCESS!

James L. Johnson

The Ministry

"The owner of an estate went out early one morning to hire workers for his harvest field. He agreed to pay them $20 a day and sent them out to work. A couple of hours later he ... saw some men standing around waiting for jobs, so he sent them also into his fields, telling them he would pay them whatever was right at the end of the day.... again around three o'clock *(and five o'clock)* he did the same thing....

"That evening he told the paymaster to call the men in and pay them, beginning with the last men first. When the men hired at five o'clock were paid, each received $20. So when the men hired earlier came to get theirs, they assumed they would receive much more. But they, too, were paid $20.

"They protested, 'Those fellows worked only one hour, and yet you've paid them just as much as those of us who worked all day....'

"'Friend,' he answered one of them, 'I did you no wrong. Didn't you agree to work all day for $20? Take it and go. It is my desire to pay all the same; is it against the law to give away my money if I want to? Should you be angry because I am kind?'"

— Matthew 20:1-15 *(The Living Bible)*

The Business

"Again, the Kingdom of Heaven can be illustrated by the story of a man going into another country, who called together his servants and loaned them money to invest for him while he was gone.

"He gave $5,000 to one, $2,000 to another, and $1,000 to the last — dividing it in proportion to their abilities — and then left on his trip. The man who received $5,000 began immediately to buy and sell with it and soon earned another $5,000." *(The man with the $2,000 did the same, but the man with the $1,000 hid it for safekeeping. When the master returned, he praised the two men who had doubled their money. But to the man who hid his $1,000, the Lord had something else to say.)*

"Wicked man! Lazy slave! Since you knew I would demand your profit, you should at least have put my money into the bank so I could have some interest. Take the money from this man and give it to the man with the $10,000. For the man who uses well what he is given shall be given more, and he shall have more abundance. But from the man who is unfaithful, even what little responsibility he has shall be taken from him."

— Matthew 25:14-16, 26-29 *(The Living Bible)*

I

The Nine-to-Five Complex

Alexander B. Simon, "B" for Benjamin, gets into his Volkswagen sedan at exactly 7:45 A.M. as he has for the last twenty-four years. It is a known fact to the neighbors in the neat, older, middle-class homes that they can set their clocks by Alexander Simon's "black bug" backing out of his driveway. Simon, owner and director of *Simon's Signposts to Glory Incorporated,* the only Christian organization dedicated to "making the message stick" through scriptural bumper stickers that glow in the dark, is a man of regularity in all that he does — church attendance, prayer meetings, board meetings. He is into the office by eight, home again by six; his lawn is done once every ten days, the hedge of mulberry shrub clipped every two months during the season, and his black VW washed and polished every other Saturday. Alexander Simon has made punctiliousness a spiritual virtue, so that even the newsboy knows now that the *Tribune* must be on his step by seven o'clock every morning.

Alexander B. Simon is fifty-six years of age. He is a

man of medium stature, kept trim by a swim at the "Y" every day at noon and a walk around the block every night before bed; white hair and steel-rimmed glasses give him that "intellectual look." His personality is classed as "gregarious with elements of dogmatic authority syndrome" according to the Berneuter Test he took as a kind of joke at a business manager's convention he attended some years ago. That test also revealed other things that Simon does not mention, such as "symptoms of overprotectiveness regarding what he considers his own ideas, a martinet attitude toward those subordinate to him, and a tendency to be irrational under pressure combined with a penchant for avoiding areas demanding major decisions." The test actually was a valuable insight into a man who, before going into "Christian business," held seven pastorates, not one of which he held for more than two years. It taken seriously, the test could have saved Alexander Simon one of the most painful experiences in his life and in the lives of other people associated with him. But Simon laughs off all such "tests" on the grounds that "God alone knows what I'm like, and I'm glad He alone really does, and whatever I can hope to be is strictly His will and His pleasure."

That business convention also gave tests on managerial leadership profiles, and Simon scored only 19.5 on a possible 50 points. If he had taken that seriously, he would have had the clue he was looking for as to why his company has such a high turnover of people, even in key "executive" positions. But to Simon, this, likewise, is "irrelevant," because "God does not run His work on the basis of tests, nor choose His leadership on man-made percentiles, but strictly on the basis of *spiritual* qualifications." Which he, in turn, lists categorically as "not many wise, not many noble, are called, but God chooses the foolish things of this world to confound the wise...."

And, of course, Simon, with that kind of snorting

laugh that dismisses social and business research as "gimmicky," points to his own "business" that has already in twenty-four short years reached well over the million mark in *net* sales. "Not bad for a one-horse outfit that began in my garage on nothing more than fifty dollars and a prayer." Which is to say that Simon points to this as "unequivocal proof that when God runs His own business with the people of His choice, nothing — absolutely nothing — stands in His way."

And who can find the necessary purchase to argue with him or even to disagree? For Alexander Simon constitutes that breed of Christian leadership who have amalgamated a general biblical and spiritual philosophy of labor with a demanding business nomenclature and have, on the surface at least, come out equal to and even better than some secular businesses. For Simon, his own "success," which he is quick to add is "by God's own goodness alone," has come from that embryonic beginning in the garage to what has to be a record, as he puts it, of the "miraculous interventions of God and a record of answers to prayer that ought to go into a book some day."

And rightly so.

Meanwhile, people in the suburban community of Waldon, population 36,000 "and growing," know him as that "kind of person," a booming laugh, a buoyant attitude about life and God, generous in his giving, outspoken in his Christian testimony, a father of three girls already through college and on their own, taking their place in the "faith I taught them," and husband of a wife who is "quiet and reserved and a peach of a woman." He is known for his frugality, attested to by the "conservative" VW's he always drives when he could be driving a Cadillac, and which he calls his own idea of "proper stewardship responsibility"; his home is a remodeled old colonial, adequate but not lavish; his own salary is "under $20,000 a year," he reminds his own "vice-presidents now and then," and adds that he has "not increased that substantially in ten years despite God's prospering of the business." For Simon, "dedication and commitment will bring their own rewards of God, and they aren't in terms of dollars and *sense*." That, by the way, is his favorite sermon topic, and he's preached it, as he recalls with some pride, "at least 118 times at Christian Businessmen's Luncheons all across the States." He serves on the boards of fourteen different Christian organizations, and gives money gifts to each of them every year "to show that board members have responsibility this way too." He manages to get a float into the Fourth of July parade every year, and for the last four years they have had the same theme: SIGNS OF THE TIMES — ARE YOU READY TO MEET GOD? Red, white, and blue bunting decorates the trailer; there's a golden plastic image of the Statue of Liberty with a boy dressed in "immigrant European clothes kneeling before it," a children's choir singing the "Battle Hymn of the Republic," and a beautiful girl reading a huge open Bible which is propped by two shaky athletes. Though the images don't all fit the theme, the community has awarded Simon's efforts with "first place original patriotic" for the last three years.

But today, as he rolls his black VW down the asphalt drive, glancing at his wrist watch to make sure he is on schedule, Alexander B. Simon, the embodiment of a successful Christian businessman, is to meet a peculiar reckoning.

For today, though it should never happen to a man of this conviction and commitment, the public auditors will confront him with the news that he is bordering on bankruptcy. Today the books will show that *Simon's Signposts to Glory Incorporated* owes a total of $657,000 in liabilities and has, including all assets, fixed and otherwise, no more than $320,000 to meet them. This includes "all paper such as outstanding accounts receivable" which comprise at least $150,000 of this.

Such news will be received by Alexander Simon with

the same unruffled aplomb of his "twenty-four years of crisis" in business. He will look at the figures, listen to the "grim realities" of his position, and then proceed to call in his "vice-presidents" for an all-morning session of prayer. For Alexander Simon will seek to meet this crisis as he has all the others — by cajoling God into the company to alter the nature of the problem and even pour in the necessary cash needed in His "own miraculous way" and thus "preserve the blessing that has been accorded hundreds of thousands of people who have used *Simon's* glowing bumper stickers to give witness to their faith."

In all of this, Alexander Simon will miss "that still, small voice" seeking to break through as it has for twenty years to no avail, the voice of God saying, "Simon, I have somewhat against thee...."

Across town and moving toward *Simon's Signposts to Glory Incorporated's* one-story colonial office building, coming from the opposite direction of the president and owner, is William R. Rawlson — Billy Rawlson — driving his 1966 Ford Galaxie that has taken on peculiar groaning and grinding sounds like a ship ready to break up in a heavy sea. Billy Rawlson is forty-four years of age, fourteen of those years given to *Signposts,* a gentle man with a gentle face. This morning Billy is thinking about the "promotion" he received two weeks ago — he is now to be called Maintenance Engineer and not simply Custodian. The new designation was given to him officially with some sense of fanfare by President Alex Simon himself who brought in a two-layer cake with red and white frosting for the whole staff to share, all seventy-eight of them.

There, with Billy standing in front of the cake in his blue overalls with two pipe wrenches hanging out of his deep back pockets, the announcement was made followed by subdued applause, for nobody, including Billy, knew what the new title was supposed to mean as distinct from the old. And President Simon did not elaborate.

Billy remembered another "promotion" he had received two years ago — which was not announced with this kind of public display, but given in the privacy of Simon's office: "because of faithful service and performance acceptable to standards, you can now order your own ammonia, cleanser, floor wax, and gasoline for the lawn mowers and snowplow...." Billy had felt genuinely overwhelmed then; after twelve years of having to have every supply purchase initialed by the president himself, this constituted a "major breakthrough" and seemed to hint that there was a kind of thaw moving into the wintry grasp of Alexander Simon when it came to wages, benefits, and "recognition of accomplishment."

But for Billy, what it had amounted to was that he could count his ammonia bottles, toilet paper, commode cleansers, and wire brushes and "maintain a proper level of such materials as befits the needs" (as listed in an interdepartmental memo from the president a few days later).

Added to that, and as some kind of seal of the promotion, Billy had been given a huge brass ring which held sixty-five keys — "one master and two copies to be worn on your belt," as Simon demanded for reasons Billy did not question. It hung from his belt now as he drove, jingling with the rattles and shocks of the Ford, the tarnished medals of the hero of "The Battle of the John," as some at the office jokingly referred to him. The ring was heavy and cumbersome for Billy, and he spent far too much time trying to single out the right key from all that assortment that fit a myriad of doors to rooms that held their own supply of multipurpose and nonpurpose materials.

"Everything must be locked at all times," Simon had warned him, "including the washrooms at night." Nobody knew why the president had such a mania for keys and locks — but it meant Billy had to get into the office early to open those washrooms before anyone else showed up. And getting sick or taking vacations was almost out of the question for him — who would open the building, the washrooms? Who would spring the locks on all those doors? Billy didn't know, and nobody told him. He suggested once that each vice-president be given a key, but this idea was frowned on by Alexander Simon as an "invitation to trouble, because supposing they all start losing keys around town — what then, hey, Billy?" To which Billy simply nodded and let it go.

Billy, of course, had expected better things here at *Signposts*. He had nothing against Mr. Simon. In fact, it was that message on "dedication and commitment that bring God's rewards, and not in dollars and *sense*" that had come as God's direct leading of Billy to join *Signposts*. He had applied for the job of Systems Engineer, as advertised, to work on the machines that stamped and bound those bumper stickers into bundles ready for shipment. Instead, he had wound up as "custodian," but he never knew why. True, his background had been strictly in automobile mechanics, but the job specification called for "no direct experience" just as long as "a man is willing to learn and has the right spiritual attitude."

Well, Billy mused now, feeling the wheel of his tired Galaxie tremble and shake as he moved up over fifty miles an hour, glancing at his watch to make sure he was going to stay ahead of the early birds and certainly the early washroom users, including Mr. Simon — well, he had to remind himself again that this was *Christian* work, and it was unlike any other kind of work. And even though his attitude was "spiritual," it apparently did not guarantee anything at all. As Mr. Simon said to him so often when he met him in the hall, like that time Billy was carrying a bucket and a commode brush heading for his daily policing of the washrooms, "We are all members of the same Body, Billy — all doing our part, right?"

27

"Yes, sir," Billy returned, but not with the same exuberance he had had in past years.

What bothered Billy now, though, was the conscious awareness of a pattern of contradictions in his life. He had become a Christian at twenty-nine, transformed out of alcoholism. He was not "a brain," but he was steady and had "a good mind for figuring out things and fixing anything that had a single working part in it" — that's the way his boss had described him at the auto shop, where he had put in sixteen years of his life. When he went to night school to study mechanics and tool and die design, the teacher there told him, "You've got a mind for design, Billy, and some of the things you've drawn here ought to go to the patent office...."

What had happened to those designs? What had happened to his ability in mechanics? Even now he knew he could work out a better assembly line for those bumper stickers; he knew he could rebuild those old machines to produce five times as many. He had even put the designs on Mr. Simon's desk once — but he hadn't heard a thing. And now he didn't know how to approach anyone of authority about what he could do, because authority was much too blurred to be sure. So he was left with the broom closet and ammonia bottles.

And beyond this was the continual battle to keep his family alive. God had been good, but mainly because his wife had managed to get a job in a diner for a few hours each night. This bothered Billy, too, because he could get additional work any time in mechanics, but *Signposts* did not allow moonlighting. Yet, it was all right for his wife to go out and work, even with kids at home who needed her.

Maybe it was wrong to think like that, Billy scolded himself. He shifted his loop of keys around so they wouldn't dig into his leg and told himself again that he was fortunate to be working in a place that had such impact on the world for Christ. Sometimes at night he would dream of all those bumper stickers coming off the assembly line, seeing them pasted on bumpers of a million cars. WHEN YOU'RE READY, GOD IS! GOING MY WAY IS GOD'S WAY! WHEN YOUR BREAKS FAIL, TRY GOD! How many people must look at those signs and get to thinking!

So now Billy whistled. It helped. Maybe ammonia bottles weren't so bad when you could be a part of a witness like that. Like Mr. Simon kept telling them in devotions every Friday. "You got to see the larger picture of souls out there who are getting it in the eye! Just think of that, and it ought to make you whistle while you work!"

So what if he hadn't had a raise in twelve years? He had a job! So what if he only took home $580 a month? He should really be counting his blessings today, like Simon had reminded him and all the others regularly. And he eased up on the accelerator of the Galaxie as the wheel started to vibrate in his hands. "This is the day the Lord hath made, let us rejoice and be glad in it," Billy said out loud.

At three o'clock that same day, Billy Rawlson would be told he was being discharged. He would get the news from his "immediate superior" Lyle Montgomery on the way to a prayer meeting called by Mr. Simon. Lyle Montgomery, who never spoke to anyone without looking at the floor, would look at the floor when he told Billy. No explanation would follow except "administrative decision and the necessity to cut back, etc., etc." So Billy Rawlson, with fourteen years of manning the ammonia bottles for God, completely stunned, would have a hymn book thrust into his hands and try his best to sing "Jesus Saves." After a while he would begin staring down at the big brass ring of keys, wondering which key Mr. Simon had held back from him — and maybe anticipating the moment when that brass ring would finally be stripped from him, leaving him totally exposed, like Samson losing his hair.

Coming on a parallel course to Billy Rawlson, at a time quite unusual for him, Morton B. Hargrave is pushing his 1970 Mercury well over the speed limit in his attempt to get to the office and to that auditor's report. Mort Hargrave is fifty-seven years old and listed officially as Comptroller for *Simon's Signposts Incorporated*. Mort has been Executive Vice-president for seven of his nine years with the company. He still does not know what that means exactly, any more than Billy Rawlson knew what Maintenance Engineer meant. Hargrave has moved around the company, from salesman, to public relations, to cost feasibility (which really meant that he had to figure "how much faith it was going to take to make a profit next year"), and finally to comptroller.

He has never been comfortable as comptroller — accounts, cost figures, analysis, monthly statements, and final audits have given him a serious ulcer. Morton Hargrave has no qualifications to be in accounting or the managing side of accounting for *Signposts*. Using an adding machine constitutes a chore, and "double entry" bookkeeping still sounds crooked to him. Consequently, he has depended on his two "knowledgeable" accountants, Milly Spade and Molly Mockinbrush, who have been with the company since the "garage days" when "the system was much simpler." Neither of the two women, both nearing retirement, know more than simple bookkeeping, adding columns of figures, posting, and handling the checkbook. The man who knows the most about accounting, Myron Downstreet, is editor-in-chief in charge of thinking up new spiritual slogans for the stickers. Hargrave pulls Downstreet into accounting once a month and has him do the monthly statement at night, paying him overtime. Mort knows and Myron knows and Milly and Molly know what's going on and that Myron should be comptroller and not editor — but then what happens to Mort? Besides not knowing "double entry" accounting, Mort also does not know how to write a complete sentence.

Morton Hargrave is not a stupid man, however. His forte has always been employee relations; that's where he spent most of his years at Sears Roebuck before coming in with Simon. Mort has been a Christian for thirty years and has always been sensitive to doing a job right. And in secular business he managed to garner a respectable reputation. He came into *Signposts* after hearing Alex Simon on the radio nine years ago "decrying the lack of good business sense in Christian organizations." Mort had smarted under that a long time, and finally asked God to show him what to do.

Mort had expected to qualify for Personnel Relations at *Signposts*, a job that was among those open at the time he had applied and which "he felt a direct leading of the Lord to try for." He was accepted on that basis by the interviewer who, unfortunately, was a young man of about twenty-three interning as a management trainee as part of his master's degree work at the local university. Within the week, Mort found himself selling bumper stickers to trade outlets over the phone. But at least his office was adjacent to Personnel, even though under Sales, so he presumed he would make employee relations in a series of devious steps through strange territory.

So Morton Hargrave dug into sales with a zest he did not believe possible in himself and a spiritual attitude that said "in time, if I'm patient, the Lord will get me to my natural station in His vineyard." And it wasn't long before he was winning customers, so much so, in fact, that he attracted the attention of Alex Simon himself. That's when the president decided the next devious step for Morton on his long road to destiny by moving him to Public Relations where he could "promote good will and positive identification with Simon's Bumper Stickers." It sounded so good when Simon told him about the move that Mort could hardly resist the job, even though he accepted with some sense of trepidation. He had never been in PR before, and he was not sure he had any of the qualifications. "No matter," Simon boomed back. "The Scriptures say that we can do all things through Christ. What do you say to that, Mort, hey?"

So Morton Hargrave found himself going to trade conventions, bookstore conventions, churches, church socials, and all kinds of denominational confabs "wherever there was space for a booth to show Simon's Bumper Stickers." He even got to the most prized group of all, the CWUW conventions (Christian Women for United Witness), a group billed as the "counter culture to Women's Lib." But Mort was not much of a public speaker. He told jokes with muddied punch lines, and most of them were ethnic jokes that offended people. He had a nervous twitch under one eye which became pronounced in front of audiences, and some of the key women in CWUW wondered what that twitch meant. He also had a habit of forgetting what he had started saying in a sentence and wound up trying to find his way back to the beginning.

After a year of that, Morton Hargrave suffered "heart fibrillations" and spent three weeks in the hospital. The PR department had to pick up the slack and finally hired a new man. When Mort returned, Simon made him Executive Vice-president provided Mort would take the vacant comptroller job which the company could never keep filled "for some reason." Mort took it, as Simon put it, "as God's reward for faithfulness" and "as God's way of providing a position in keeping with Mort's health." Mort swallowed and took it.

Now he has heart fibrillations *plus* an ulcer, and the way he was driving across town to beat Simon to the office and those audited reports was bound to start it bleeding. Mort had never come into the office when the auditors were there. He had scheduled his "annual physical" during that time, leaving Milly and Molly to work with the auditors. Somehow it had always come out all right.

But Milly had called him last night to tell him of the auditors' findings, and suddenly there wasn't enough Maalox in the house to hold Mort's stomach in place. Now, sleepless and hurting, he was trying to pray as he drove: "Lord, a man fifty-seven years old can't start just anywhere again.... You are faithful. I don't question that ... but, Lord, even You will have a hard time placing a comptroller who let a company slide into a half million debt.... Lord, I tried ... or maybe I didn't try enough...."

But even as he prayed, the seven years of playing the role of comptroller in instinctive reaction to the "survival syndrome" had already taken a masterful hold. For Morton Hargrave was already thinking of ways to make that colossal gap between liabilities and assets fit some kind of "capital adjustment." Even now as he should be facing the realities of the shambles he was so much a part of, his mind kept looking for ways to reconstruct that auditors' report to pass Alexander Simon's own untrained financial eye and shift the deficit to a spiritual level. Years of pride in successful accomplishment of his work in secular places died hard in this, of all places, the ideal setting called Christian work.

But by five o'clock that same day, Morton Hargrave would have lost in his bid to outmaneuver the auditors. He would not be discharged, however. Alexander Simon would never admit to a mistake in judgment, especially of those he ranked in his "vice-president class." Instead, Billy Rawlson would go to make room for Hargrave. And at five o'clock, the once impeccable custodian of sensitive personnel relationships at Sears Roebuck, the "Executive Vice-president of *Simon's Signposts Incorporated,*" would be offered the new job of Supervisor of Maintenance.

And long after the office was quiet and empty, Morton Hargrave would sit at his comptroller's desk with a bottle of Maalox to rethink his fortunes and God's order in the cosmos.

One of the few people who actually knew what was going on at *Signposts Incorporated* was already in the office at 7:00 A.M., ahead of Billy Rawlson. Pearl Munson, Director of Personnel Relations, had only five years in at *Signposts*. Yet her ten years with a Madison Avenue advertising firm in New York had given her a keen eye and ear for company structures and "those little creaks in the system that usually spell a weakening of the dikes somewhere." Pearl has not been a Christian more than seven years. She is thirty-eight years old, a pleasantly plump woman, fairly attractive, with naturally blonde hair and "motherly" blue eyes. *Signposts* has this one center in Pearl Munson that keeps the plaster from coming down in one big splash around Alex Simon's head. For it is Pearl Munson to whom the seventy-eight employees look when they unload their frustrations and confusions; it is Pearl to whom they go for a "redress of their grievances." It is Pearl, who has the responsibility but not the authority, who must listen to the vexation of department heads, rank and file employees, and even vice-presidents. The problems of "inequity of wage scales, of performance overlap, of misplaced and displaced people, and of failure to weld the people in the company into a workable unit" have all been unloaded on her desk.

Pearl has no answers for all of these imbalances. The man who does is not interested in the "carping of people who look for perfection in everything" but only that the "product, the Good News, not be jeopardized." She has great admiration for Alex Simon, for what God has been able to do through him to bring *Signposts* from that inauspicious beginning to a level of production that a lot of secular businesses could not emulate. She has sympathy for him too — because she knows that the big man is not capable of controlling a company that has grown beyond the reach of his limited talents in administration. She knows that he knows that he is failing in his command, but rather than admit it he continues to fight on to maintain "what God has given to me as a responsible steward, for which I must give account some day." Pearl Munson would give anything to help him see the way to do that, but she knows that for Alex Simon to ask for help of that nature would be to him an admission of failure, and with that admission God would be less to him than He promised He would be.

Meanwhile, knowing all this, Pearl Munson has stayed. Though a constant flow of departmental memos comes into her office complaining of disorganization; though the morale among the people moves to a staggering low; though the communication with Alex Simon is mostly an exchange of spiritual amenities which he wants to hear; though the company itself runs a bumpy ride day after day threatening to pop every rivet in one grand, glorious collapse; though even the coffee breaks don't do much to ease tensions or weld a sense of necessary fellowship needed among the people; and though many times there are increased evidences of questionable ethics in promotion, financial transactions, and "product performance problems for the consumer," she stays on.

Because Pearl Munson hangs onto the vision, if not seen in the warp and woof of the company goals — which are nonexistent — certainly in her own mind and heart. She stays because she sees the potential inherent in this God-given ministry-business or maybe business-ministry. She is not wholly convinced that spiritual bumper stickers will make any profound impact on the state of man's spiritual life, but she is certain that the simple slogans could be expanded to a level of publishing that could eventually do that. She stays, cultivating the hope that Alexander Simon will come to see that his business is not to be run like a church congregation at a Sunday school picnic, but as a complex manufacturing concern in need of careful planning to conserve people and materials for the highest good. She maintains the optimism, as feeble as it is at times, that the president and owner will realize that his *first* responsibility is to the people God has given him for the vineyard. For Alex has not yet realized that the image or blessing of any Christian product is dependent upon the attitude of the people responsible for it — that they must believe in it, sense involvement in its ultimate intent, and be excited about what every day can contribute to its effectiveness.

As for herself, Pearl Munson has found a sense of fulfillment in *Signposts* that she did not have in a secular firm. To be a part of a final product designed to confront man with spiritual reality, as nebulous and marginal as that might appear, is worth all the problems and pains that go with it. At least so far. But only, of course, if there remains that hope that the potentiality intrinsic to it can be realized — that there are horizons to reach, mountains to climb, and the leadership to spur people to attain those goals. So during her five years here she has maintained her cool and given others some reason to hope, some points of navigation to lay hold of in the ever-widening circle of confusion that is *Signposts*.

But she has to admit that deep within she has taken on the steady pulse of pain as she has fought to hold some balance. She knows that Myron Downstreet should be comptroller of the company, not editor; she knows that Morton Hargrave should be working in personnel with her or even doing her job, rather than suffering in accounting; she knows that Billy Rawlson's record indicates that he could do more for the company in the engineering department than in custodial; she knows that most of the people in the company are manning positions for which they are not suited. She has made her changes in hiring policies, putting in aptitude tests and seeking in every way possible to match the job with the man. But all of it has come to nought — for Alexander Simon has his own method of "placement" in keeping with his "years of developing a God-given intuition and insight about people that you'll never find on tests." And so it is Pearl who must reconcile the high turnover in some jobs; the loss of young, creative, spiritual minds; the gradual but deadly deterioration of spirit in men like Morton Hargrave and Billy Rawlson. Lately her protests are kept in silence, for there is no way to discuss these matters with Simon, who considers the employee turnover "God's sifting of men's hearts."

Yet Pearl Munson stays, ever hopeful, ever optimistic, clinging to the thin bark of God's all-seeing, all-knowing attributes, believing that in the end He will right the system.

But today, at twenty minutes past seven, the auditors' report has spelled out the terrible dimensions that twenty some years of mismanagement have accumulated. Even as she hears Billy Rawlson's rattling Ford pull up outside her window, she knows the Lord has visited *Signposts* with a summons. Even as she hears Morton Hargrave's quick, nervous steps down the hall heading for his office and the confrontation that is about to cripple him, she realizes that *Signposts* has come to a moment of truth.

And it will be a day of suffering for her too, for she knows that Alex Simon will demand that people be cut from the payroll. Since "the product is of primary importance and people are expendable in God's eyes," it will seem the easiest and most rightful route to take to stem the outlay of cash while trying to close the gap between commitment and resources. It will be up to Pearl to decide who will go — should it be the young, creative minds who are necessary to keep up the pressure for change so desperately needed? Or should it be the old who must be turned out after years of faithful service, forced to face the bleak reality of not finding employment in a market that never has tolerated age? She will not make the decision about Morton Hargrave or Billy Rawlson — Alex Simon will do that through her assistant Lyle Montgomery, known as the "man from Glad." But it will be up to her to notify the others, the same people she gave hope and cheer to in the dark hours. She will work feverishly into the night, calling people in other companies trying to place them — for the young she will have no problem; for the older, it will be a long night indeed.

But today Pearl Munson will also put her own position into jeopardy before the six o'clock hour. For when Alex Simon demands payroll cuts and declares pontifically that "we have lost our spiritual bearings.... God is calling us back to mend our ways...," it is Pearl who speaks up for the first time in months while the six white-faced vice-presidents sitting in that sacred semicircle around the president's desk look on aghast: "It is nothing spiritual at all, Mr. Simon... it is strictly a case of bad management... and if we could ask God to forgive us for that and start afresh to do it right, we won't need to fire anybody...."

And so it is done. Alex Simon gives her one sidelong glance, shuffles his papers on his desk, clears his throat and says, "Let's pray." The prayer does not touch on mismanagement, of course — instead, it is a plea to God that He "save His own witness; that He overrule the forces of darkness surrounding us; that we do nothing now in the flesh; that we stand aside to see You work and get glory to Yourself...."

Thus endeth the first day of the beginning of the darkness that covered *Simon's Signposts to Glory Incorporated*. And the Lord looked on all that He had made, and He proceeded to move to Asia.

II

The Problem

No, God does not abandon His own, even when the creative process He has spawned is marred or distorted by the clumsy attempts of His deputies. That is probably all that *Signposts Inc*. really has going for it now — apart from those like Pearl Munson, of course, who will stick to the ship even though the sails are in shreds. In a real sense, God will have to live with it, at least until Alex Simon finally realizes that all this upheaval is intended to get him to correct course before he piles up on the rocks. The future of *Signposts,* then, hangs on what Simon does in the critical days and weeks ahead. And it is in this peculiar time-lag that even God Himself is victimized, for He can only communicate His intent to minds open and sensitive to what He is trying to say. Alex Simon cannot hear yet, or see. Whether he will or not in the time he has, nobody can tell. For he is a product of a culture of certain complexities, certain mind sets, certain spiritual bents — a culture that does not, mysteriously enough, allow leadership to admit error or even contemplate the possibility that a certain course has indeed been a wrong one.

It might be said that the experiences tangent to *Signposts* are certainly not indicative of Christian organizations as a whole. Of course not! Thank God for some who have learned their lessons early. But even though *Signposts* is a fictional object lesson, the symptoms pervading the "structure" are not. Too many of these characteristics already grip church business operations in a paralyzing stranglehold, some to a greater or lesser degree.

It can also be argued that any organization must have the right to trial and error, the right to do it wrong, the right to stumble along hoping to find itself. This is also admitted. But what is in question here is that there is a peculiar frenzied attempt to ignore the wrong as wrong, to cover the wrong with an overlay of what is "right" and thus to complicate the entire human interpersonal relationships which cannot by themselves know how to correct it. Any organized effort in the name of God may falter, have its false starts, have its "day of reckoning" perhaps; but there need not be the devastating dereliction evident in *Signposts*, the deliberate avoidance of a consideration of what is spiritual and what is practical business. There need not be that destructiveness of the human spirit classified as that "expendable" part of God's work. There need not be confusion of purpose, dissipation of energies, and poor motivation: these are not absolutes that must accompany a work of God "where two or three are gathered together." There can be disenchantment without demoralization; there can be disagreement without deterioration of spiritual attitude; there can be complaint without an ultimate conspiracy to storm the head office to "get heard." There can be an order to Christian work, a sense of continuity, a feeling of movement, a cohesiveness despite individual differences.

Well, where is the problem? Why is it so few actually

attain the ideal which is certainly within reach under God? Why are there so few Christian organizations that strike their own happy note, as evidenced in those who work within it day after day?

The blame cannot be put on Alex Simon alone, although any organization is only as strong and successful as its leadership. And even though the analysis must begin there, it does not end there. For one thing, Alexander Simon is but a product of the culture that spawned him, shaped and bent him from his adolescent years in a "godly home where no one questioned authority," through his seminary years, his church pastorate years, and finally his business years. He is a product, not of willful dereliction in any sense, but of costly omissions in his childhood family education, as well as his formal education. He has been taught that the simple categorical statement is a cure for all ills, and he has sought to project this in all of his relationships. He is not alone in any of this.

But the problem goes to every level — not only to the Alexander Simons, but to the people who serve in *Signposts* and every other Christian concern like it. The line worker's attitude toward his work is as much in question as the department head's. The problems are a mixture of complexities, from too much idealism on the part of the worker to too much presumption on the part of the leader. There are problems involving a proper philosophy of Christian work: when to consider it a business in matters of proper remuneration in wages, pensions, insurance, sick leaves, etc.; and, of course, when to consider it strictly a ministry in matters of interpersonal tension, authority figures, complaints, arguments, disagreements, and what to do about making changes that need to be made without posing a threat to the "big man in the chair." There are complex attitudinal predispositions in the "institutional" worker who has known nothing but Christian work all his life, as opposed to the worker who has come "over" from the secular world and who is quick to recognize the disparities and insufficiencies of the strictly "spiritual" overlay on the structure.

There are problems of personality struggle produced by the realization that this "ideal community" does not meet the expected dimensions. There is the nature of Christian ideology, which is no absolute, but a product of tolerated weaknesses of leadership, which often breeds mediocrity in production and acceptance of equipment and materials far below the standards of excellence. There are serious problems with regard to a proper view of money: whether profits are legitimate in Christian product orientation, the problem of honoring contracts and sales agreements, and just simply paying bills on time.

There are problems of Christian ethics in advertising and promotion: how much to promote and to what extent, always being careful not to cross the line into exaggerated representations, although this occurs nevertheless. There is continual stress as to how much of the world's methods ought to be incorporated in a Christian product image, how "glowing" can you get about Scripture bumper stickers to stay ahead in the field.

There is the problem of people who cannot see the ultimate impact of their labors on others — this is not unique to Christian work, but it is far more critical in an organizational ethos that emphasizes "team work" in facing the world of lost men and women.

So there is no such thing as a "one-dimensional problem" in the function of a Christian organization, which is often classed as purely spiritual. There is a complex weave of stresses, some more intense than others, but all rooted in the unwieldy merge of hard-nosed business realities with the spiritual ethic and accompanying sensitivities of people who cannot determine which of these is to get what emphasis at any given moment of the day.

But in all of this, there is a solution, thank God! To find it, however, takes analysis. And it would seem only logical to begin with the Alexander Simons, the conceivers and energizers of the entire mosaic. Therein lies a picture of both courage and culpability — but in seeing them one can better understand the complexities innate in the Christian organization and even the frustrations and farcical experiences that often attend it.

The Problem of Culture

To examine Alexander Simon is to examine a goodly number of the "owners" and "presidents" of Christian organizations. Again, certainly not all of them fall into the mold, but the composite is there.

Simon's boyhood was centered in a Christian home. He "took Christ" into his life when, as he says, he was five years old. He doesn't recall the day, the time, or what he did or said, but he adamantly insists that he *knows* it was then. At the age of twelve he "went forward" at camp to "rededicate himself" to God for His service.

The pattern is not unfamiliar to many in the church. The validity of such encounters cannot be questioned, but the historical, absolute fix on these nebulous dates seems a flimsy base for an entire life's journey. For when Simon says of these spiritual mountaintops, "I never had a doubt since," there emerges an element of personal pride that indicates a major flaw, a refusal to admit human frailty lest it negate the "legitimacy" of these experiences. To Simon, Christianity has not been a journey filled with "ordained stops" where he could reflect on the genuineness or lack of genuineness of his Christian walk; rather it was one grand leap from spiritual embryo to the grave, a zipping shot of high adventure, moving from "glory to glory," bulldozing the enemies of God as he went.

Beyond this, what was to shape him more directly, and perhaps more pertinently to his future as a Christian organization leader, was the presence of spiritual authority symbols through his early and later adolescence. The

"God figures" filled his life from Tiny Tots to college graduation, demanding total obedience, total abstinence, and total surrender. His father controlled the dinner table with a Bible on one side of his plate and a leather strap on the other.

His pastor controlled him in church with a long bony finger with "thus saith the Lord" on the end of it, carrying the awesomeness and finality of the glaring black eye of a shotgun barrel.

His Sunday school teachers poured the total array of "God's government" across miles of flannelboard, from the bloody wars of the Jews in the Old Testament to the sun turning to blood in Revelation — and no questions allowed in between.

His camp director posed a "God figure" of athletics, who rewarded individual achievement with seconds on hamburgers and a sermon on "humility" and who masterfully controlled his world of sleep, play, thought, and even blocked bowels with a skill that had to be supernatural.

His choir leader taught him the disciplines of "listening for the flat notes in those around him as a kind of protection against the distortions of heavenly harmony in himself," but he never learned to detect flatness in his own treble.

His counselor at Bible school, a bachelor going on forty, warned him in his freshman year that "God alone controls the sex organs and they are to function solely on procreation." Which meant God was watching carefully, ready to judge any indulgences in the natural pleasures, whether by act or by thought.

The careful regimentation practiced within those sacred walls seemed to be designed to make certain he had no temptations in that regard. He learned to fight all "urges," all "torments," as being a "ruse of the devil" and went through repeated daily rituals of surrender, begging God to "take his glands and neutralize them."

The sense of "sexual prohibition" as being "forever

declared in heaven" was to show up later in his organizational "rules of the road" which covered hemlines, hair styles, make-up, and formfitting attire which "had to be in keeping with the spiritual decorum of a Christian organization." What that "code" was to do more than anything else was to bring an unholy self-consciousness of the body as an evil composite of glands that could self-destruct at any time, depending on the thought, and wipe out a half-dozen unsuspecting male production workers in the process.

The proscriptive aspect of sex was given double-barreled significance in his developing authoritarian role later on as it coupled with the imbalanced sex image in his family. From the earliest age, it was his mother who assumed the task of teaching him the moral and spiritual values of Christianity. Consequently, all Bible figures, including Christ, took on a peculiar feminine aura reinforced by the church government that reflected the "power lobby" of feminine legislation. The male role, by apparent voluntary acquiescence, was confined mainly to taking the offering or driving the bus — and in his last year of junior high, a woman took that over too. The Sunday school, choir, missions committee, banquets, bowling, and badminton all showed the majority control of the female. His father, preoccupied with "the more essentials" of business and commerce and weekends at the lodge, was content to allow the imbalance, oblivious of the confusion that was building in the emotions of his own son who longed for masculine heroes in Scripture to be cast by masculine instructors. Though Simon was to find a shaky balance in his sex role later on, the dominant feminine influence, together with a deep-seated suspicion of his own sexual function at times, was to force him to excessive displays of masculine authority with women in his own organization. To "assert the rightful role of Christian manhood as a fixed life in the Apostolic Succession, a man must assume command." This was to show up in the deplorable wage scales for his women employees and also, even more critically, put Pearl Munson, the one person who could have saved him, beyond reach.

For Alexander Simon, the intersection of his adolescent life by these authoritarian figures — even these few — was to shape him for what leadership he was to assume in the future. Along the way, of course, and fortunately, God managed to squeeze in between the press of these powerfully influencing absolutes of power and remind him of "love, joy, peace, longsuffering, gentleness, goodness, kindness," against which there is no law. And there were those times — actually the safety checks on his life — when Alexander Simon experienced the genuine euphoria of true spiritual encounter. If these had been taught to him early, and the attendant models of such behavior impressed on his mind, a godly humanism* would have been his bent, and his contribution to the Kingdom of God might have been much different. But as it was, the symbols and models of authoritarian God figures always came to the surface, finally to lay the total cast on his character:

No Questions — that indicates a seed of unbelief.

No Personal Rights — that constitutes carnality and rebellion.

No Discussion — that smacks of argument with God.

No Defense — that connotes a spirit of negativism.

This extreme credo of his life drawn from his early church culture, whether by intent or default, was to form the basis of his relationship with God and finally with others. This might have been tolerated — if one would allow that much — in the pastorate or even on the mission field where freedom of movement allows some escape from the press of such code. (But even on the mission field the pressure of "God figure" syndrome can have a devastating effect, especially when the per-

---

Humanism in terms of human perspective in interpersonal relationships and values, not in theological sense.

sonnel are locked to a fixed territory or term of service with no possible way for relief.)

But when this is carried into a complex organizational structure of seventy-eight people thrown together eight to ten hours every day within the confines of pressuring Christian-industrial enterprise, the results are predictably disastrous, barring a miracle of God. (The lack of miracle has to be that God simply wants no part in sweeping up behind willful blindness.)

What compounds the picture even further, of course, is the low educational profile Simon has to support his role as leader of a complex business. Like so many in key positions in the Christian organization structure, he pursued a "Christian education" to prepare for "Christian work of some kind, whatever the Lord reveals." The problem was not that he pursued a Christian education — he would need that too — but that he allowed that short span to be the total input for his "future ministry." He had his drill in theology and knew God's relationship to man, but he had little or nothing on how man relates to man, and that would be the critical factor in his later life. But the Christian school put predominant stress on "ministerial careers," not on business or anything else. And perhaps rightly so. If a graduate was to find himself pursuing or even "led" to other careers, even considered "ministerial" but demanding a wider spectrum of training, then some kind of godly sixth sense would have to take over. Or else, even more logically, the man ought to pursue whatever education necessary to qualify him. So Simon, while being thoroughly equipped theologically, was totally lacking in his understanding of the business, bureaucratic, corporational "vineyard" he was to conceive. Without even the sketchiest profile of the psychological, social, and communal drives of Christians committed to his charge, the "good ship evangel" which was *Simon's Signposts to Glory* was to begin its voyage with tattered sails.

The fact that at no time in his training years or even

"executive emerging years" did he seek to find out what his personality and aptitudinal line was with regard to leadership and organizational or business detail spelled out how strongly entrenched Simon was in the concept "I can do all things in Christ." When he did take one of those tests "just for kicks" at a business convention ten years after *Simon's Signposts* was on its way, it showed that his interests and aptitudes lined up most closely with "diamond cutter" or "pipe fitter." To which Simon would only guffaw and comment, "Just goes to show you how ridiculous those things really are." What the profile also showed was that his ability to relate to people was extremely low and that his social proclivities were more in keeping with a groundhog's in February. That was to be borne out later in his poor rapport profile with his own rank and file. Actually, if the tests had been taken earlier, and if he had been counseled as to what they meant, Simon could have found the resources to add to his low administrative aptitude. There are many aspects of leadership and business that can be learned, as many a "pipe fitter" will testify.

But again, for Simon, "when God calls you to do something, He also provides the necessary equipment" constitutes an intractable stance in his life-style credo. It would show up later, too, in his "rule of thumb" for personnel selection which was based "on more godly instinct than job description and job credential." So what *Signposts* was to be noted for was that the wrong people were in the right jobs, supra-talented people in the supramenial jobs, and the one-dimensional types in the multidimensional jobs. Management to Alexander Simon is summed up simply as "a matter of making sure everybody knows who's boss — after that, do your job making a joyful noise unto the Lord."

Can it be said that Alexander Simon does not constitute the norm but the peculiar exception in Christian leadership? Perhaps. But that is not the point. He exists. What it says is that every Christian leader, if he is to analyze himself at all, has to take his fix off that composite figure. The question is whether the shadow of that dimension still hangs long over each leader's respective life style, or, hopefully, is it diminishing? Any culture has its effect on all who pass through it. Simon got the full one-sided dose, and he is not alone in that.

Let it be said, however, that the fault is not Simon's in total. On him lies the indictment of refusing to evaluate himself honestly in terms of his increasingly emerging role as leader and failing to listen to what God might say to him with regard to his needs as custodian of His treasure. On him lies the final charge of indulging willful ignorance regarding himself and the purpose of the organization God had allowed him to construct. But the "God figure" fully cast is hardly capable of owning up to possible flaws in the divine architecture.

Beyond that, however, the real fault, if it can be traced, lies with the culture that spawned him, at least that slice of it that led him to believe that the patriarchs were no more qualified for their "jobs" and thus there was no reason to put credence to "cultivating management skills to do the Lord's work today."

The culture that whispered the line that the "authority figure" or the "God figure" covers for a multitude of sins must finally stand in the dock, if a culture can be put on trial.

Perhaps the fault lies in the enshrining of the "called" rather than the "called and the fully prepared." The blame lies, if anywhere, with the indoctrinators of that culture who continue to perpetuate the myth that a man's abilities do not count finally in the conducting of God's business, but only his willingness and zeal.

It lies, too, peculiarly enough, with the constant reference to the Scripture that "not many mighty, not many noble, are called, but God has chosen the foolish to confound the wise" as being ample proof that God puts priority on stupidity in order that His hand might be seen in the conducting of His affairs among men.

It lies even more so with those who still teach that it is not *how* Christians conduct their business but *what* is produced in the end. In other words, a million, glowing, spiritual bumper stickers a year cover a multitude of *willfully* clumsy, inept, disabling administrative peccadilloes of Alexander Simon? Unfortunately, or fortunately, depending on which side of the authority line one happens to be, God does not wink at the means which have been used to justify the ends.

Therefore, it can be concluded, Simon can be excused by the forces of culture which shaped him and over which he had no control. In a sense, yes. But he is also at the age of accountability. It will not excuse his evasion of that accountability or the necessary annual inventory-taking of his own spiritual and administrative stock. Culture shapes, but self-awareness reshapes, and the resources of God are ever available for the reconstruction.

Of course, not all Christian organization leadership falls into the mold of Alexander Simon's adolescent spiritual upbringing, nor are they all sunk so intractably into the mire of spiritual calcification. Some Christian leaders are naturals, instinctively attuned from birth for their mantel of responsibility. And yet, interestingly enough, they are the first to admit that they are still "working at it." Others, with less instinctive flare for the task, have learned to empty themselves periodically and thereby to draw freshly on what God provides in the total educational world to "fill the gaps." But there are the Simons, too many of them, who still labor under the grand delusion that the "kingdom and the power" are automatic benevolences bestowed on them by God at the moment of commitment. These, as already shown, present strange enigmas to the body.

To probe further, it is noteworthy here that in comparing the experiences of those Christian organizational leaders who have proven successful with those who have not — success being in terms of the attitude of the people who make up the group — it is apparent that the problem does find its roots in the *authority* versus *authoritarian* syndrome.

Authority that cannot command respect by leadership dynamic or credentials or expertise often shifts to authoritarianism out of a "fear of being found out." Where abilities are lacking, insecurities evident in relationship to that, and the complexities of the organizational function too difficult to cope with, the "leader" often will resort to authoritarian postures in order to save what he can. Because for him to admit to limitations or incapacities for "corporate" problems is but to contradict the "God figure" image.

Erich Fromm, in his book *Psychoanalysis of Religion,* put it this way in explaining the authoritarian personality or syndrome that applies, as well, to Christianity when wrongly interpreted for collective enterprise. "The essential element in authoritarian religion and in the authoritarian religious experience is the surrender to a power transcending man. . . . The submission of the mind overwhelmed by its own poverty is the very essence of all authoritarian religions whether they are couched in secular or theological language. In authoritarian religion God is a symbol of power and force; He is supreme because He has supreme power, and man in juxtaposition is utterly helpless."

God has much more in mind for the Christian, however, as Fromm suggests as well. The Christian yields to God as rightful *authority,* but not as *authoritarian* who takes everything from man and gives nothing back. Rather, in His *humanistic* relationship to His own (as Fromm declares), God as authority — commanding all resources and riches and gifts — gives to His own that His own might in turn give it back to Him in joy.

More specifically, God in His humanistic concerns put the precious gifts into the employees of *Simon's Signposts;* it was up to Simon, then, as custodian of them, to bring out those gifts to share with the outside world. Had he learned that early in life, perhaps he

51

would not have followed the "patriarchal line" of an almost totalitarian rule. He should have learned early, in any case, that it was one thing to command a mob of disorganized, displaced Jews who demanded the absolute in command to save them from themselves; but it was and is quite another to mold and shape talented, intelligent, committed people, God's people, into a productive unit for His glory! It is a difficult task and should not be entrusted to novices.

As it is, Simon simply moves on the experiences of his past and gradually assumes the image of the Theocrat-Autocrat, although he would not know what that was — that is, ruling with absolute, unlimited authority as divinely guided. He becomes that "God figure" incapable of mistakes, limitations, and bad judgment.

In all of this, it must be said of Simon that he does not deliberately seek to be that way. He sincerely wants "to be fair, well-liked, and respected." He truly "desires to be God's man for the hour," and in some instances, there is no question that he is. But the tragedy of it all is that none of these "sincerities" carry him far enough to affect his own spiritual organizational custodianship. Instead, he becomes a truly marginal man. As Paul put it, "That I would want to do, I cannot; that I would not do, I do." This he would not admit to anyone, not even to his wife, hardly even to himself. And on this perhaps spins the fortunes or misfortunes of *Simon's Signposts Incorporated*.

How is it then that Simon should, with all these limitations and gross shortcomings, "be chosen of God" to conceive and lead *Signposts to Glory?* Perhaps the question will always have to lie in a theological or spiritual conundrum answerable only in Glory.

Perhaps, more accurately, it has to be said that God is not taken by surprise in the whole economy that He alone engineered. But the emergence of the Simons — with all their poor credentials and lack of fitness for what they insist they must do — is not an element grinding against the flow of God's traffic pattern in history. It is but a classic example of the mystery of God's grace where He is willing to tie Himself to the clumsiest shapes of clay in the hope that some piece of the history He has willed will come to pass without the chemical mixture blowing a hole in the universe.

It is an example, not of God *confining* Himself to the foolish deputies, but rather His *condescension* to work with even the smallest ingredients of *desire*. It was the *desire* of Alexander Simon, his urge to intersect the line of God's projected track for history and become a part of it, that God honored. Whether the world needed bumper stickers that glow in the dark was not the issue. God saw a man struggling for "his place in the sun" and moved accordingly to allow him that journey. In the end, He had to hope that the Word, slapped on a few million automobiles and plaster walls, would not "return void."

The exaltation is not for the Simons, who are permitted to make their connection with the line of God's history, but for God and God alone. That God would be *willing* to put His own hopes on so obtuse a human dimension is what drives the philosophic sages out of their minds. But at the same time it is this very fact that keeps the hopes of His own alive.

However the question remains: Is God victimized or exalted in this Christian-industrial enterprise? Is Simon's "desire" enough? Can God really get into the picture that already shows such damaging distortions? If He condescends to follow the stumblings and authoritarian rigidities of Simon, will He likewise follow him all the way into *Simon's Signposts to Glory Incorporated?*

This may never be proven by the examination of the ingredients that follow. But it may leave something to ponder.

III

The Organization– The Incredible Journey

Alexander Simon got his "revelation of *Signposts*" while riding down the expressway in Queens, New York. He had been watching the illuminated billboard in the distance, becoming larger as he approached, until he saw the letters in green luminous blocks: YOU'RE IN GOOD HANDS WITH ALLSTATE.

At that point something "clicked in his mind," he recalls. "I suddenly saw millions of red balloons with green Scripture verses on them flying over the Great Wall of China declaring that God still had the whole world in His hands...."

The "click" may well have been the sound of the firing pin in his brain hitting on wet powder. For after fourteen years and seven pastorates, Simon had come to the point in his life when "something had to happen; God had to show me where I belonged." Whether he had "failed" in those seven pastorates would never be admitted. "Failure" was not a part of Christian service.

But if he had then "been a saint out of place," he had arrived there because of his predictable need to have his hands on every meeting, every coffee-klatsch, every cell group. With most of those churches running a marathon schedule, Simon literally "ran out of gas" the first year. Besides that, each church had one immovable "personage who kept a single eye on the parsonage" and whose "God-given sense of authority" was equal to, if not better than, Simon's. The final shoot-out always went against Simon, because he was never capable of making the decisive point in any confrontation.

Simon's "wilderness journey" through those churches became a trail of empties, people who had listened and tried to hang on to his dried-out messages with stoic forbearance, but who succumbed to the hollow winds sweeping through their barren, unfurnished minds and souls. No one would have been more eloquent in supporting Simon's need for "something to happen to him" than they. Or maybe it was just that he was not "pastorate material."

Meanwhile, the "click" really turned out to be the sound of a broken firing pin as far as the balloons over China was concerned. Nothing really discharged. A whole year of barnstorming the country for his "balloon evangelism" netted him exactly $920 from "interested souls." With that he printed up 5,000 red balloons with green Chinese lettering spelling out John 3:16. But the prevailing winds do not flow constantly in a single line from Waldon, Connecticut, to Red China. So finally one Sunday afternoon he launched the balloons over Chinatown, New York. The fact that they landed in Harlem was really not so disastrous. "The Word has gotten out ... and whoever gets those balloons will be curious enough to want to know what the Chinese says."

None of this in intended to disparage Simon's intelligence or sense of purpose. There are many "balloon projects" in the Christian world launched on far less a foundation, many of which have not yet found a resting place in the target audience. What it illustrates, though, is the tenacity of Simon's *desire* to cut into the line of God's will for mankind and get his assigned vehicle. For such tenacity, one simply has to pause ten seconds in silent salute.

At any rate, the pursuit was rewarded three months later when, on arising one foggy morning, Alexander Simon was confronted with a blob of bubble gum stuck to his back car window, put there as a Halloween prank. At that precise moment, as he thought of what to use to scrape it off, the "click" resounded in unmistakable detonation, the report that had to be heard around the world. Simon's "bumper stickers that glow in the dark" had leaped into his vision off the stagnant trampoline floor of his brain. Whether it was right for it to emerge from such a misshapen clump of despicable waste is immaterial. It is but one more object lesson of what God can — or maybe must — do with a child of His whose imagination is colorful enough to translate the lowest images of life into the "ideas" that will gross millions while confronting "mankind with a solid spiritual witness."

On this does the church and civilization advance.

On borrowed capital gleaned from second mortgages on "everything from the house to the cat," Alexander Simon began his venture in his garage with a second-hand bumper sticker casting machine and a worn-out wife who had by now about succumbed in that cross-country race through seven churches. But with true grit and grim hope that the race might now be ending, she gamely manned the glue pot and prayed that the "Lord would have mercy on what they appeared to be about to do."

One year later, through "the miracle of God," the forging of each painful step of their "ministry" had become a "company" of six people. The familiar green bumper stickers with black lettering treated with luminous chemicals were to show up everywhere in Waldon, whether welcomed or not, so that flying over it at night the community seemed to be a "throbbing spectrum of greenish fluorescence never at rest." *Simon's Signposts* was to become a bane or blessing: either to be sworn at by outraged car owners who did not want to be drafted into being advertisers for God and who fought to scrub off the gummy label; or else to be literally worshiped by local Christians who saw this as their opportunity to witness without the "painful, time-consuming demands of direct confrontation."

On these two pressure points of consumer behavior, *Simon's Signposts* began to grow. And it must be said that beyond the bizarre overtones of its questionable genesis, there was intrinsic to its fabric the heart and soul of a man of God who was out to "find his niche." Though the effort was fumbling and stood on a shaky premise at best, the Word was, after all, becoming mobile by gum-label tenacity. And perhaps at that point God was willing to take what He could to affect a confrontation with man despite the capsizable pitch of the launch.

At any rate, *Simon's Signposts to Glory Incorporated* was born. The garage became the matrix for the miracle and sweat. For Simon, the "company" had become his altar. Whereas he had "been misplaced" in the pastorate, he now controlled his own "church." Whereas he had missed in his missionary balloon venture, he was now making connection every day with the lost, "making the message stick." He had indeed "intersected the line of God's will and would share in His history." Selah!

But even now, with his "magnificent six," the "ministry" was taking shape out of the tracings of his own predawn concepts of structure rooted deep in the building of the Tabernacle. The "ministry" was his, born out of his mind, sealed of God ("we're making expenses, which is proof enough"), and entrusted to his careful stewardship. It would rise and fall on his capacity, or lack of it, to preserve and protect. Nothing, therefore, escaped his eye or hand. He was everywhere, casting, gluing, binding, sealing, loading, and even delivering — and "sticking wherever a smooth surface dares to expose itself." He was the first to arrive in the morning, the last to leave at night. He alone had the keys to whatever needed to be opened or closed.

Already, even in the simplicity of the "ministry" in that garage, Simon saw himself as the axis. All the others, including his wife, must revolve around him. They were, in the end, expendable commodities, taking last place in the priorities of the *product* that "must not, at all costs, be hindered from its appointed destination."

If such a stance was grating to those around him, it did not show itself in the embryonic environment of the garage. To his loyal few, his omniscience was expected, even anticipated. At that point in history, all of that was diluted by the intimacy of their relationship in the total "ministry." They could work and laugh, cry and pray together, and the ever-present shadow of Alexander Simon over them was but the symbol of God Himself.

It was there in the simplicity of the "garage ministry" that the model of Christian enterprise was articulated the best. There the people worked "for the blessing of it," unconcerned for the primary financial returns. There the fulfillment of seeing the Word of God riding the flesh pots of contemporary society was enough. There the one-dimensional flow of operations, uncomplicated and undemanding, provided the milieu where Christian work perhaps ought to remain. There, in no more than eight hundred square feet of space, people bumped elbows, and rubbed shoulders, and melted into a unit forced upon them by space and the common, easily known and understood purpose. There, too, was where Alexander Simon could find fulfillment and where his "calling" could best be served. There he commanded manipulated, controlled and was undisputed "authority." And in the place of centrality, he could do all that without resistance. He was not unloved for it. His stance of omniscience and omnipresence did not constitute en croachment on individual rights or freedoms. The simplicity of the environment begged no structure of command, no complicated communication systems. In this "ministry" Simon was a laughing, portly man known for his kingly benevolence. Perhaps, then, this is where Christian industrial enterprise ought to stay, bound in the euphoria of its "ministry" with men who are eager for work, ready to sweat, and all out for the Cause.

But it was not to be.

On a wintry morning five years after the *"Signpost* revelation," Alexander Simon woke up to find that his company had a net profit of nearly $90,000. He had now come to the line that stands between Christian "ministry" and "business." He thought. Money and the accumulation of it was God's way of saying to Simon, "Come up, come all the way up." Money means blessing, and blessing means success. Success then means "expand, enlarge the borders, for there is much land yet to possess."

At that point, one could wish that Simon would have paused long enough to contemplate seriously what the crossing of that line would mean. One could wish that he would have looked beyond it to the tangled barbed wire of business and what it could do to choke off the "ministry." One could wish he would have begun to see that he was about to step over into a new world of taxes, depreciation, administrative transfers, employee benefits, insurances, public audits, sales, advertising, capital gains, product image, and all that had to come in the new order of the Christian business. And in the seeing, hopefully, he would think seriously about his capacity to negotiate that maze.

At this point, however, all men are most vulnerable. Simon the Christian was no different. The momentum of his cause had rocketed him to unbelievable heights. God had worked the miracle. To retreat from that moment of entering the "Promised Land" was but to "go back on his vows." The possibility of turning out 30,000 bumper stickers a day, nearly triple his current production, was too much to resist. Today Waldon, tomorrow the world!

Now, Alexander Simon became a fragile figure indeed. One could pray for him, although with some conflict. On the one hand, the temptation would be to ask God to provide a "timely slip on a banana peel" to give him second thoughts. Yet, knowing the bent of his "God figure," nothing would hold him back. Prayer for him, then, had to be for what lay ahead, the world that poses the greatest of all challenges to would-be captains of their own destiny — the demands of negotiating a ministry that has become a business, a business that somehow must be kept in the context of ministry. Now would come the demands of trying to rule by the "Beatitudes" while trying to balance the books on the scale of hardnosed work performances. Now would come the many confusing hours of not knowing whether to pray or cry, and even his carefully manicured life style would bring him to the brink; whether to write off thousands of dollars of "bad debts" inflicted by the "brethren" or seek legal redress; times when the demands of "sales promotion" would bring him dangerously close to breach of ethics; times when he wouldn't know a "quiet place" except in the john; times when the demands of his "product" would rise to curse him.

For Alexander Simon was about to cross over to a reckoning with devastating truth that has plagued others so much like himself; he would no longer be the minister, but a "president" of a business; and while the Rotarians would love him, the Lions revere him, and the Daughters of the Revolution ask him to speak at the Fourth of July celebration each year, he would also be fair game in the jungle of free enterprise.

Whatever "ministerial protection" he may have had up to this time, it was now about to be stripped ruthlessly from his back. Whatever idealism he may have maintained in terms of God running his business would now begin to take second place to the unsympathetic demands of the apostles of commerce. Whatever "vineyard" dimensions he envisaged for those who would work with him and for him — mostly *for* him — would be jarred loose unceremoniously in his first battle over wage scales. Whatever dreams he carried about the saturation of the nation with Simon's spiritual bumper stickers would become nightmares in the ugly spectre of competition that would imitate him, outproduce him, and outsell him.

Whatever tolerance and admirations he may have experienced to date from his "consumer public," who viewed his product as "harmless and perhaps in public interest," they would now turn on him with suspicion and criticism for his "unholy profiteering in God images."

One could wish Simon would have seen all that before crossing the line — noted the "giants" for what they were. One could wish in that reflection — if he had allowed it — that he would have taken the greatest single act of godly courage in his life — refused it! Or if not that, at least measured himself against the awful pitch of the mountain he would have to climb and sought to add to his "virtue" those things that make for strength. Because what awaited him would demand far greater acumen in leadership and business than he now possessed.

Courage, tenacity, relentlessness, dedication, and spiritual fortitude carry a man of God just so many miles. In the spiritual world they can cover for the lack of expertise. In the business world they land on the mean blade of the dog-eat-dog scramble, and there is no quarter. The lions do not close their mouths to the Daniels in that arena. There is no second time around in that world, and recourse to spiritual rationalization is but to beg the point.

It would have been well, then, if the church fathers had taken note of the man who now stood at the line. It would have been well if they had laid their hands on him and anointed him for the incredible journey he was about to undertake. It would have been well if the saints had gathered around him then, even as the angels must, to surround him with unction.

It might have been well if he had listened to his wife at breakfast, who dared to break the years of imposed silence regarding her husband's decisions and said, "Simon, mark well what you do this day."

But, true to his life style, Alexander Simon made his decision five minutes after swallowing his bacon and eggs. The crossing of the line was done with dispatch, marked only by the change in size of his accounts ledger.

The Incredible Journey

Alexander Simon was to move from his garage to 10,000 square feet of one-story rambling red brick. The structural design that would allow for proper traffic patterns and office layouts that would provide enough light and ample production space "were incidental to the design." For Simon, the "symbolism was of paramount importance." Even the flagpole's place in the three-acre plot demanded days of concentration, and it took two weeks and six moves of the fifty-foot white pole before it was decided that it should stand off the rear parking lot in full view of the president's bay window. Anyone facing Simon in his office would see that pole with its Christian and American flags and have "no doubt as to where this company stood."

The entire "decor" of the inside was designed to capture and emphasize the "spiritual nature of the organization." Praying hands were ubiquitously evident, even in the rest rooms. The head of Christ done up in two-foot murals hung in every office cubicle, with gothic lettering underneath that read: THE SILENT LISTENER TO EVERY CONVERSATION, THE OBSERVER OF EVERY CONDUCT. Paintings of biblical scenes showed up in other "strategic areas" or wherever there was wall space that would tolerate them.

The point was, as Simon put it, "anyone coming in

here from the outside will know immediately where this organization stands."

Unfortunately, the assessment of that from those on the "outside" would be more in terms of the company's reputation in finance and the integrity of its claims with regard to the product.

For those on the inside, the excessive predominance of the "spiritual reminders" was not, of course, considered objectionable; what it did say was that there was a herculean attempt to make certain that no one forgot for a minute that all that went on within these sacred walls was "spiritual." What was to finally develop was a steadily rising resistance to the fact that those who worked for and had commitment to *Simon's Signposts needed* this reminder, as if somehow without the steady gaze of Jesus day by day they would run amuck in their thoughts or actions and seriously damage the temple.

Simon's attempt in all this was to cushion the organization at the outset against the shocks of secularism that had to come knocking on the door. It was an attempt to diffuse the hobgoblins of mammon and declare to the world that this indeed was holy ground. It also said that Simon was still carrying the "garage ministry" syndrome, and every attempt had to be made to make certain the company did not slip over the line from its simple spiritual dimension to the mundane business jungle. This was still his "church," and he would choose the congregation. For him, the "organization" was only in name, not in structure. It was still a kind of spiritual retreat house, and he would run it as such. For Simon, it was to be an attempt to ignore or head off the demands of the corporation and even to keep all matters of strictly "business" at bay with a covering of spiritual gloss.

It also pointed up the conflict within the man himself, a conflict that has to be sympathized with: the desire to manufacture a product for public consumption without losing the spiritual euphoria that goes with it — or to allow a business-ministry without bowing to the demands of business. The conflict was to run through the entire warp and woof of the organization, driving executives nearly mad because of the spiritual mandate that prevented them from facing the practical problems in practical ways. Eventually, on some days the entire rank and file could hardly wait for the five o'clock whistle. They were desperate to escape into the world of reasonable, or at least near reasonable, circumstances of cause and effect.

Even such simple matters as backed-up commodes and chronic breakdowns in electrical power or machinery — even the coffee maker that poured out colored water and not much more — were put into a "spiritual frame of reference" which might have some "spiritual lesson." If a man had to wait for the "spiritual lesson," then the correction of the malfunction was often delayed too.

Case History

Much later in the life of the organization, Billy Rawlson, the maintenance man, reported a malfunctioning in the heating unit and asked permission to strip it down a little at a time to find the faulty part.

"This will save us having to shut down the whole unit and maybe even save us an overhaul," Billy advised.

SIMON: You are so sure you can find it, Billy?

BILLY: No, but I'd like to try.

SIMON: Maybe the Lord will find it, Billy, and keep it running without our taking the time?

BILLY: Well, maybe, but —

SIMON: Let's test Him on it and see....

So it was left. A week later the heating system broke down and had to have the major overhaul. The staff had to work with their coats on in the February cold, thus cutting work production by 50 percent. To all of this, Simon was to say, "Well, maybe the Lord had to teach us to appreciate heat in the building, after all...."

And who can argue with it finally? And granted it may seem picayune at best and could be tolerated on lower functional levels. But when the symptoms of the same spiritual overlay begin to control top-level decision making where the lifeblood of the company is at stake, the effects of it can be critical.

Case History

With profits sliding somewhat, Morton Hargrave, the comptroller, had worked out a plan that could possibly offset it. Presenting it to Simon, Hargrave said he believed it would work.

SIMON: I take it you've prayed about this?

HARGRAVE: Well....

SIMON: (sensing hesitation) Is it God's solution, Mort?

HARGRAVE: I think the proof of that will be in how it works in the market —

SIMON: Mort, the proof of God's will is in how certain you are that the solution is His. We've got to remember that this is a business, and it hangs closely on how sure we are that what we propose to preserve it with is fairly fail proof. I suggest that maybe you should pray a little longer until you are sure this is a workable business principle.

Morton Hargrave went back to his desk somewhat confused. However, he decided to try his plan anyway, figuring he couldn't lose in the effort.

Three months later he was back in Simon's office, literally ecstatic over the reverse of the profit slide his plan had effected.

SIMON: Before you get too carried away, Mort, remember that we are a *ministry*. We don't crow about money around here. The minute we start chalking up our profit successes, we're in trouble with God.

What all this is really rooted in, of course, is Simon's inability to cope with the "corporate structure" side of the business, which has forced him into a much more articulated role of "spiritual leader." Rather than admit to the limitation and hire a vice-president for corporation affairs, he will continue to pose as the image of total knowledge and forever force the complications of business matters into an unworkable spiritual oversimplification.

He is not alone in this, nor, again, without sympathy. There are a goodly number of top Christian executives who, realizing the overwhelming demands of the task which is beyond them, will seek to put a "spiritual screen" over the inadequate performance levels. The same is done in secular work, except the rationalizations are formed naturally from different timber.

But in a Christian organization, where the ideals of the rank and file are so high, where admiration for superiors is already established, the exposure of this "habit" is bound to have devastating results. What happens eventually is that department heads learn to "play the game" in like fashion, and the domino effect takes place all down the line. And all of this is accompanied by a growing sense of disorientation on the part of the unsuspecting who suddenly find themselves caught in a spray of "invocations and benedictions" for no particular reason.

Other such cases will be discussed later, but the important point now is to realize that the shape of an organization is a direct result of the *administrative* weaknesses or strengths that were brought into it. And God will not perfect that which has been ignored, especially when the cure is readily accessible at the local business college. On top of that, of course, is the already defined spiritual extremity of the authoritarian syndrome which, of course, becomes more and more rigid as the ability to cope with corporational complexities becomes less and less. Weakness of rank and file can be worked out and perfected, but only as there is capable leadership knowledgeable enough and self-experiential enough to detect them. But the problem of how to affect those of the "main cog" is even more complicated.

So now Simon had come into his own with his concepts of what he should be as a leader of his own "corporation" already beginning to flex its muscles and rise to a "significant movement within the mainstream of the church," which leads them to the more serious area of his concept of what the organization is. Peter F. Drucker, outstanding teacher of successful management, in his book *The Effective Executive,* has basic propositions of organizational function that can be put back to back with Simon's at this point. Though Drucker discusses the secular corporation as such, his tried and proven principles are fit measurements for Simon's organizational corporate necessities. Structure does not change from secular to spiritual; the ingredients for success remain the same. It has nothing to do with "ideology" and remains a separate level of consideration.

Drucker's concepts of organization will point up some of the giant false steps taken at the outset by Simon, who sought simply to make his "corporation" a spiritual one, totally negating the necessity of facing the burden of the strictly organizational demands.

1. *Drucker says that the executives or organizations seek to bring in people who will "contribute" to that group as a whole* — Simon seeks those who merely "function" in a job; contribution is what comes later in terms of "souls" intersected by his spiritual bumper stickers. The emphasis is counter to the kingdom principle of the Son of God: He chose people first and then developed them to their fullest capacities that in turn the "product" would have its fullest impact.

Further, the principle of bringing people in to *contribute,* in the total sense, to the organization and ultimately to the product places a responsibility on Simon to make certain every employee committed to him finds his potential and is encouraged to give it in a true spirit of desire. This is that *humanistic* principle, referred to earlier, versus the *authoritarian*.

To develop *contributors* in the fullest sense takes time, know-how, and most of all a sensitivity to them as persons. It requires an attitude of responsible stewardship to the individual first, the product last. This holds true for the Christian organization even more than the secular, simply because God expects it and amply demonstrated it by His time spent with His disciples. But Simon, schooled more in the expendability of people, is not prepared for that.

2. *Drucker states further that an organization needs "commitment to values and their constant affirmation" which is usually "something that the organization stands for."* It was not simply bumper stickers which Simon considered paramount. His "values" were actually summed up in his handbook "Conduct Guiding Employees of *Signposts to Glory*," especially one paragraph that was to show up on various signboards in "key areas":

> "In keeping with the proper godly demeanor, employees will refrain from whispering, gossip, unseemingly boisterous laughter, and modes of dress and general comportment that contradict the purity of God's calling."

This concept of "value" was bound to create strictures to such an extent that one employee commented, "A man can't even pick his nose unless he goes under the desk."

"Values" for the Christian worker go deeper than the superficial overlay of prohibitions. For him, they are directly related to a sense of participation in the ideals and goals of the group. Too often in Christian organizations the sense of "goal" is summed up by the rank and file as the "length of the line between your desk and the rest rooms." But when the true "value" of goals in the highest sense is articulated, the worker realizes that he is a critical part of the total operation and that everything he does, no matter how small, goes toward the ultimate intersection of some soul with the message of God. "Values" to the Christian worker are in the fulfillment of being a part of the Cause, of sharing with like minds in the total task, of being willfully locked together in work and fellowship that sees personal development while fulfilling the passion of God. It in no wise means an absence of problems, tensions, or frustrations in the course of that fulfillment — but where there is a proper "value system," these problems do not remain permanent nor are they likely to burrow deep into the mainstream of motivation and purpose.

Simon presumed this sense of "value" to be automatically resident in each employee, when in actuality his task was to articulate it — not simply in the regimented devotionals, but in model behavior. Simon could have begun to "articulate" it by the attention and emphasis he put on the worker for the task. Emphasis on goals and regular sharing of what the total effort means or has meant to people outside builds "values," and in a Christian organization the failure to take that into account contributes to poor motivation which but reinforces the sense of mere "functionality."

Again, a Christian organization, as Simon should have learned but didn't, is unique in its purpose. It is not conceived simply to buy and sell a product, nor to operate in terms of "market" alone, but to develop the people involved to their highest potential in terms of their gifts and contributions through their proper task orientation which, in turn, leads to their spiritual maturity and fulfillment.

When asked what they think their "sense of value" is to the Christian organization, most workers will comment along this general line: "It's a job." Or, "I don't think I'm really that important." All of which says that they have learned to accommodate themselves to their "value" as set by the company, or director, either directly or indirectly, which is that they are merely piece workers hung together on restrictive codes. If mediocrity is to be explained at all in the Christian organization, it has to stem from the empty "value system" of taboos and internal behavioral circumspections. "A man can spit into the wind," the old philosophy has it, "but it is a law of negative counterforce that says he will have it back again." A Christian organization whose "value system" spins around negatives will find the group spitting into the wind rather than with it. This is bound to bring questionable returns. As rustic as the analogy may be, no culture, whether it be the organization or the community, has been successful in perpetuating itself on what it is not.

If Simon had learned to practice the art of humility with his own department heads, together with honest self-evaluation, the true values would have taken shape and ultimately passed on to the rank and file. Instead, Simon would "practice his humility before God and God alone." Sharing the products of self-evaluation or honesty with his vice-presidents would only "lead to a weakening of command." His leadership, then, was cast in military terms. He was not concerned with the group entrusted to him, but with the state of the profit and loss statement. His leadership was designed to "protect the image of God," to "maintain the lines of authority" which turned out to be a structured code to preserve and protect the church. Nobody expects a Christian leader — especially those in the group under him — to become maudlin in his confessions or repeatedly display attitudes of self-crucifixion. That only breeds disrespect and unreality. But somewhere between those extremes lies that demeanor which is essential to the positive "value system" of the Christian vineyard principle.

In other words, Simon missed the necessity of model behavior as the most significant point of his leadership role. Consequently he had by-passed the very spiritual truths flashed abroad in his bumper stickers. Christian workers, perhaps more than their secular counterpart, are sensitive to the emergence of "false values" based on contradictory images. They have come to expect much more. When these false values continue to go unchecked, they whittle away at the respect until the organization becomes the subject of mean, caustic jokes. It is at this point that the organizational group ceases to be what God intended — if indeed it ever was. It may remain busy, functional, and even "productive" on the measurable graphs, but the brass has already replaced the gold in the temple.

3. *Drucker goes on to say that the "immediate task of the executive is not to place a man; it is to fill a job.... It should be task-focused and not personality-focused."*

Simon, on the other hand, in his concept of organization, does not select people on the basis of what they can do, but rather on their "proximity to the doctrinal and spiritual standards of this organization and their willingness to be loyal to those standards." What a person can do, then, is secondary.

Simon's spiritual absolute may bring the "right personalities," in his terms, but productivity, personal achievement, and sense of well-being will be minimal or absent. For this reason, many Christian organizations flounder in the confusion of "low task proficiency," and it is one of the main reasons why so many in the organizations have that "hangdog" look. It is partly a kind of paranoia, a constant looking over the shoulder for fear of being caught "doing what they don't know what they are doing." And it is partly a look of apology for not putting in a decent day's work for the indecent pay.

Case History

In interviewing a job applicant for the position of "graphics manager" at *Signposts,* Simon was to talk to a young lady who carried considerable job credentials. The "credentials for the task," however, were not his major concern. What he looked at first was her "theological profile," among which were questions on the "Genesis gap theory," pretribulation and pre-millennial posture," and "dispensational versus nondispensational flow of God in history." She had not filled in these "critical areas," although her full page of conversion experience at the age of nineteen was certainly "valid enough." What resulted then was a thirty-minute "crash course" in "doctrine on which this organization stands," after which the young lady was given a "fundamentals of the faith primer" which she was to read and then face those questions again. Not once up to then had Simon even alluded to her "graphics profile."

She completed the "theological section" with no real sense of resistance, since she was willing to do "what was necessary to share her life with God in this place."

After that, the conversation went like this:

SIMON: I see that you earned nearly $14,000 a year with Standard Graphics of America. (Pause.) Well, you should know that a Christian organization cannot come anywhere near that. I could see $8,500 at the most. You see, as a Christian organization we are dedicated to other things besides money. Being dedicated to God means we are fully His, and we make our sacrifices accordingly.

GIRL: Excuse me, but may I say that I was fully dedicated as a Christian even as an artist for American Standard Graphics —

SIMON: Yes, but you see, it's different with us here, isn't it? Here we are *full-time* Christian workers, and a good part of our time and energies are *given* to God. It's the vineyard principle which you do not fully grasp yet, but it will come as you grow with the company.

GIRL: You'll forgive me for my misunderstandings then. But if I understand correctly, coming into your organization means I must reach a new level of dedication, or at least different, which will be substantiated finally by a 50 percent cut in my salary?

SIMON: (awkward laugh) Well, you know in the Scriptures that Jesus gave a penny to those who started at eight and a penny to those who started at four-thirty. We've come quite a ways from that. But the fact is, Jesus was saying that money is not the issue in the vineyard; it is the proper spirit of dedication. Besides that, you see, we have a certain wage scale that is set for female workers of our company —

GIRL: I see ... what you are saying now is that there is a certain level of dedication, beyond the other, which is according to sex?

SIMON: (another laugh) Well, like I said, these things will all become clear to you as you grow with the company....

Simon but demonstrated then his own penchant for seeking "correct spiritual personality" as primary, as over against the necessary selection on the basis of "task orientation." He would develop a "kind of spiritual nepotism," pulling in the "spiritually correct people" (which of course was his right) at the expense, too often, of individuals properly qualified for the task. In the end, in the name of "dedication" he was even to demonstrate his own rationale for his measure of the female workers as being forever fixed in the scale of the economy of God.

That girl, fortunately or unfortunately, took the job "out of curiosity to see just how much I was to grow with the company." In so doing, she would find herself abandoning her sensitivity toward her role as a "graphics manager" and become instead the "dedicated nine to fiver," working constantly toward a "right spiritual attitude toward her skills" and less and less on the actual results. She would inevitably follow the pattern of others of her sex, even as Pearl Munson, reduced finally to production without creative control or disciplined art as the "task" actually begged. Low salary, low status in the "organizational chart" (where women usually landed), and low profile of final contribution would have to be compensated for by the knowledge that "dispensationalism, millennialism, rapturism, and creationism were at least settled for the record." And beyond this, of course, the "euphoric experience of knowing I was a full-time Christian worker."

4. *Drucker added that "it is the duty of the executive [director] to remove ruthlessly anyone — especially a manager — who constantly or consistently fails to perform with high distinction. To let such a man stay on corrupts the others.... Indeed, I have never seen anyone in a job for which he was inadequate who was not slowly being destroyed by the pressure and the strains, and who did not secretly pray for deliverance...."*

Simon's declared "selection principle of employees on spiritual requisites rather than task" already is bound to evade many critical "performance standards."

But to Simon, the spiritual principle now having to be carried out to the performance proficiency element is summed up this way: "Anyone who is called to this Christian organization is bound to it, and God alone has the authority to remove him. It is our duty to make certain that a person who is not up to performance is given proper spiritual counsel to make certain nothing stands in the way of God's perfect will for him in the job. We are, after all, a ministry."

Though this sounds compassionate, it really constitutes an inability to accept the fact that the "spiritual personality" could be incompetent for the job. Rather than face it as a "task problem," Simon will seek to garnish it with the irrelevant (at this point) spiritual solution. What this ultimately breeds is unrealistic tolerance for mediocrity and indolence. It makes a shambles of the total work performance, because all jobs are locked together. The tolerance of poor work performances in any one spot, in the name of *spiritual responsibility,* is bound to shake the work force's confidence in the soundness of the leadership. If each man's work performance or task is conditioned on the other, then there is no way to save the morale on purely spiritual rationale. If a person with a record of incompetency is not to be fired, then at least his resources should be evaluated to determine where he might fit in the organization. But to ignore the performance and hope to make spiritual counsel the final cure is to allow a peculiar erosion to permeate the entire structure.

5. *Which leads to one final critical point of Drucker's, that "the effective executive does not make staffing decisions to minimize weakness, but to maximize strength.... Organization is the specific instrument to make human strength redound to performance while human weakness is neutralized and largely rendered harmless...."*

For Simon, it is the opposite. He will shift people in his organization on the basis of their weaknesses — the spiritual attitude always coming first, then the matter of skill — thus "avoiding any further difficulties that might arise."

When Drucker says that "the organization can make a man's strength effective and his weakness irrelevant," he is not saying that the director is blind to weakness. His responsibility to use the strengths of any single employee in accounting, for instance, is done so, bearing in mind his inability to get along with people. But his strengths become the basis for the task, because in staffing on that principle, it assures a greater sense of morale on the part of the worker in his awareness of being used "for what I can do," rather than being "shuffled around on the basis of what I cannot do."

It is a peculiar commentary on the Christian organization that the "strength" of its rank and file is seldom, if ever, computed in the total organizational evaluation. Most Christian workers have an almost morbid sense of their "failures" or their "inabilities" and seldom conceive that the organization gave them a new awareness of their skills. Instead of seeing Christian work drawing from their strength base as God-given for the good of the company, they see it only too often as "a fantastic X-ray probing for the smudge prints inside the apple rather than pointing up to the 90 percent edible part of it."

Staffing from weakness is to show up finally in Alexander Simon's inability to recognize achievement properly, to compliment for work performance, or to publicly inform his entire group that their efforts are noted in the progress of the company's profits and production. The results of this organizational aberration are the total stripping of motivation and a floundering in a lost sense of purpose. The fact that Christian workers in Christian organizations seem to have to apologize for it says enough.

Perhaps these five leadership concepts are too few to clarify completely the disparities that exist between *Simon's Signposts Incorporated* and the tried and proven principles of effectiveness in secular corporations. But they at least show that the Christian organization under the Simons has begun on a shaky premise at best. And they certainly point out more clearly how difficult it is to mesh the spiritual with the business demands, to move the "ministry" into the "corporation level." They show how important the leader is, perhaps even more than in the secular counterpart. They emphasize the point brought out earlier that the task of the leader in this milieu demands a man of specific gifts or at least broad training, not only spiritually, but in such areas as social-behavioral science, psychology, and group behavior. They also indicate that such a man must be endowed with some leadership ability and that this is not automatically endowed the moment the responsibility becomes his.

This, of course, brings up Simon's view regarding the

"gifts of the Spirit" as taught in 1 Corinthians 12. For him the entire passage lends itself to his own spiritual bent, and the reference to "differences of administration" means that God will bestow upon him whatever is necessary, regardless of whether his natural ability ever equips him for it. The idea being that once a man becomes a Christian, God will reconstruct the total man, ignore whatever natural bents he has or does not have, and pour on him all the new equipment necessary for whatever task to which he is "called." And there is credence to the rule that in the ministrations to the Body of Christ often such gifts are "added." But it becomes a precarious rule of life and experience to presume that God will ignore the opportunities for a man to equip himself through available means or circumstances. It is one thing to draw on the "spiritual gifts" for the edification of the Body. It is quite another to presume to have those gifts for the complexities of a corporation or business that demand peculiar acumen for negotiation in a world not attuned to the spiritual. To run a church or a church agency with its group of voluntary workers is simply not the same as molding diverse personalities into a daily mesh of workable units hard up against the business realities of product and profit orientation. The peculiarities and demands of such a world put a different strain and stress on the leader. It is not that the Lord is slack concerning His promises, but it simply means that there are some areas, by the nature of their complexity, where He expects His own "to make his calling and election sure." A "spiritual gift," even as listed in Corinthians, won't help a plumber "plumb" any better; it won't help a mechanic clean a carburetor any better; beyond that, it won't make a corporation leader out of a totally ignorant, unprepared, and obviously limited "garage chief" such as Simon really was. It is no discredit to Simon that he doesn't have all the gifts. And it doesn't reduce the size of God in the universe because He does not make a corporate organization man out of the simple cookie cutter variety. To force Him into that role puts a note of the ludicrous on what has to be a more logical order in that universe.

What's more, *Simon's Signposts* did not constitute an emergency in time by any means; it was conceived *over* time and allowed the man who was the axis to "add those elements necessary" for what he had to know in the alien land and environment being thrust upon him. For the gifts of healings, tongues, prophesyings, faith, etc., as listed as "spiritual gifts," are to be pursued for ministration to the "body," which is the internal needs of the church. But when it means stepping over the line into this new, strange, and taxing arena of a world hung together on the confusing array of laws and principles governing the business world, the leader had better look around him for whatever resources he can add.

It also underscores again — and it bears repeating — that the success of leadership is not in terms of how many bumper stickers go out to intersect the lives of millions for God. If any organizational leader actually desires to know his "success profile," he need but test or measure or observe the attitudes of those who comprise his "vineyard." That's where God measures it. It is seen in terms of employee attitudes that speak for fulfillment, morale, sense of cause, and sense of accomplishment in terms of the product. This does not mean that the attitude is always one of solid loyalty, or that every waking hour he is a "company man," or even that he is so dedicated he is willing to die for it. What it means is that the man or woman committed to that organization will stand by it for what it has given him in terms of finding his God-given strengths and opening channels for him to communicate those strengths to the outside. This is not innate in him. It is to be infused by the leader by his acts of concern and the lines upon which he rests his organizational ethos.

It says then that the daily "business" or "activity" or "hum" of organizational machinery does not automatically mean organizational health. Certainly not in the Christian corporation. What this analysis says thus far is that the organizational life can sometimes best be seen as being present or absent in those who sit in the regimented company devotionals every morning at eight. That simple confrontation, seen in true light, can either be a devastating revelation or a satisfying reinforcement that the pain and time taken to "lead" for the highest good of the individual has not been wasted. It even says that when the "health" of the Christian organization is seen in the attitudes and motivations of the individuals as being voluntary and self-perpetuated in line with the leader's care, the *regimented* devotion is no longer really necessary.

Further elaboration of these principles will come later in the solution summary sections, but at this point Alexander Simon, having missed any of this along the way, continued to progress in predictable fashion in his "authority figure." His own rank and file learned to peg him early within the definitions of the "Theocrat-Autocrat."

At any rate, the "God figure" is cast. Alexander Simon has mounted the bridge of his "good ship evangel" called *Simon's Signposts to Glory Inc.*

So now what of the "crew" and that "nine-to-five complex"?

IV

The Group – I Only Work Here?

"However far you trace our history," says Antony Jay in his *Corporation Man,* "you find groups: not just the family group, but something larger.... This simple primate grouping, however, is only half the story. ... it is the other half ... that makes us different from all the other primates, that has profound implications for the modern corporation."

Mr. Jay goes on to explain that the primary group that moved together from the first staggering beginnings of man was called the "hunting band." This group moved collectively for defense and food gathering, mainly for self-perpetuation. Mr. Jay points out that "employees and managers of large corporations have been formed into what they are by a half a million generations in the hunting band."

But beyond this, and particularly critical to the role of the Christian industrial organization within the so-called "church group," Mr. Jay points out that the key to the large corporation's success as a "hunting band" is the emergence of the "ten group." It is this "ten group"

— usually made up of ten people — that, as Mr. Jay points out, "the modern corporation or any large organization still depends on for survival."

The church in itself is not a "ten group" by its very nature. It is a "hunting band," as it were, needing the "ten group" people who by their close associations in regular patterns and bound by the common objectives of survival are able to give the main "hunting band" the directions it needs.

The church is a group made up of various personalities who confront each other in voluntary activities across limited periods of time. The "church group" is primarily a "contact group," and whatever should come of that contact is purely up to the individual's desire to "follow up."

The same can be said for the "mission" as a group. It may pose the structure of the corporation as such, but it must depend on the "ten group" emergence within church culture to maintain its purpose, direction, and expertise. Though it may suffer some of the problems of a corporation as such, it is still so revered, even idolized, that the mistakes, miscalculations, sometimes even bad financial management and failures can be glossed over under the hero image. The mission group is an extension group of the church, nurtured purely by her motherly instincts, provided for by the collective responses of the members and somehow looked after in old age when the armor is laid aside. The pressures of security, future, job failure, and job accountability are absent; the missionary lives in an enviable, independent culture unto himself as a ward of the church. He may fight his peculiar problems attendant to that, but he does not have to own up to the stresses of the "corporate structure" that demand total accountability for time and money spent.

But both the church and the mission, as "nonprofit religious corporations," are not "survival groups" in themselves. They depend on some "ten group" inner core that by collective operation and model activities continues to exert the kind of influence, directly or indirectly, consciously or unconsciously, that affects the continuing viability of them.

Despite the often staggering ineptitudes, the bad management, and the peculiar caprices and poor leadership judgments of the Alexander Simons, the Christian-industrial organization is *potentially* — and it probably remains purely *potential* until the Simons alter their own courses — constituted to exert "ten group" influence.

It does so — when fulfilling its objectives intrinsically welded into the framework — by being a catalyst for the entire "fellowship" and extension ministries of the church. Though it may not be a model in organizational structure or even stature, it does possess a modular image, the bringing of people together in collective working units to produce a product for mass consumption. The fact that it manages to straddle the world of business and commerce with "the message of the church" and project to areas the church, in its strictly voluntary work force, could never hope to reach, poses a facet of success that the church dearly needs.

What's more, even though the organizations under the Simons seem to stifle the resident expertise, they still provide people who, by their everyday experiences in negotiating the pressures of a business-ministry, are in some measure equipped to put some necessary balance into the often "unrealistic" internal structure of the church itself.

And there is no question either that a good amount of the moneys needed to plow into the extension ministries of the church come from the profit surpluses of that organization.

Ultimately, the only barrier to the Christian organization becoming the model "ten group" is not that the expertise and creative energy are absent, but only that the leadership has not learned to use them to their fullest potential. Again, there are some who have come to that peak, and there is no question at all that their influence is already felt, though the church may not be aware of it.

The point to be stressed here is that the church has not taken the time to understand this. If the church is, in fact, a "hunting band" within its spiritual cultural context, she can only come to a "corporate level" — using the word loosely — as she takes into account this "ten group" catalystic potential in the Christian-industrial organization. Whether this "taking into account" would mean commissioning services for company presidents and even rank and file is a point worthy of discussion. But beyond all that, it would seem that the church's ignoring of the organization as if it were some kind of retarded child in the family is only adding to the "dwarfed mentality" already experienced there.

The lack of such consideration, then, plays a significant part in the "complex" the Christian organization man brings into his job. Too often the church considers him as one who "failed in his calling" to the mission field, pastorate, or teaching. He is often looked upon as one who is "out of place," having failed to rise to the "proper priorities of evangelism and church growth." To the church, then, the Christian organization has emerged only to give this "displaced person" an opportunity to "reintegrate himself into some useful function for the church and society without which he would find it difficult to make a go of it."

Interestingly enough, the church at the same time takes the opposite view with regard to Christians involved in secular business, holding them almost in the same sense of awe as the missionary, for "it takes considerable tenacity and courage to be a Christian in that arena." And it might even be said that Alexander Simon could be classed as one — along with others — who, having failed in everything he tried, found "redemption" in his *Signposts to Glory Incorporated*. But to charge all who serve in that context as being of the same genre is to do them a gross injustice.

The Christian organization, then, poses a group situation that is unique to the church voluntary agency. It straddles both the church, in its charismatic role, and the outreach projection into the main stream of secular man. Because it is distinctly different, never totally owning up to a sense of "ministry" or "mission" in the popular sense of the terms, it comes under suspicion, or at least poses an enigma — the enigma too often being centered around the "profit making" enterprise that it encompasses.

But meanwhile, the record should be put straight for those "nine-to-fivers" who must suffer this "complex" at the very outset. Let it be said that the Christian organization man is an individual with "gifts" considerably different from those of the missionary, pastor, or teacher — but certainly not less than these. The fact that God is willing to overrule or even tolerate the fumblings of the leadership of these groups seems to be an indication of His desire to give those individuals opportunity to share those gifts with the world. And in the granting of that, the church's "spiritual mandate" reaches far beyond to the borders that the voluntary agency could never penetrate.

And yet no one has paid more dearly for that privilege, or even "sacrificed" more in his sense of "call" to provide the world with a confrontation with God, than the Christian organization man. No one exhibits more tenacity to stick with an often "bad situation" for the Cause than he; no one displays more attributes of tolerance and forbearance for poorly managed, poorly structured organizational functions than he; no one has "died daily" more often over the anxieties of personal compromise forced on him by the contrary dimensions of the business-ministry or vice versa. No one, having committed himself to the peculiar caprices of the Alexander Simons, has experienced more "contrary winds" nor felt the bite of contradictory attitudes about profits, product images, and sales graphs than he. No one — and this is unique to him — fights the battles he does trying to fit the business into a "ministry mold" as dictated by the president while being driven at the same time to make the "ministry" pay. No one puts any more hours into prayer or suffers more agony and sweat or spends half as much midnight oil to sort out the "insane happiness" of a typical day's work than he.

And yet, for all of that, he can manage to stay sane for his family, teach a Sunday school class, serve on six boards to help other floundering organizations like his own, chair missions conferences, sing in the choir, and still somehow "stay sweet."

Granted that there are those in Christian organizations, like others, who carry no credential and are not "models" of the true behavior as listed. But for the most part, those who carry on their struggles to right the balances in these corporations, who have given of recognized talents, skills, and expertise — recognized in terms of the business world — must be justly reckoned with. In a sense, they are rare people who, knowing the disparities, despairs, and incongruities of working within the Christian organization, knowing the peculiar disrespect they are often held in by the church — which is mostly an ignoring of them as not significant for the "larger picture" of outreach — they stick it out anyway.

Meanwhile the "complex" that materializes within the Christian organization can only be seen in the people who comprise it. Webster's dictionary defines "complex" in two particular ways, as used here:

"Complex has to do with a system of repressed desires and memories that exert a dominate influence on the personality ... or a group of obviously related units of which the degree and nature of the relationship is imperfectly known."

Together with the "complex" too often developed before he gets into the organization, the organization man must now face up to the added, more confused level within.

To understand it one has to look at the man himself in his various motivational garbs, including his "call":

1. *The Christian Conditioned Institutional*

The Christian Conditioned Institutional, or C.I. as he is known here, has come into the organization along the same route as Alexander Simon. For him, his life from the "age of five," or perhaps early adolescence, has been a carefully nurtured journey filled with the same dominant images. For the most part the C.I. has known Christian institutionalism that has kept him within the "friendly confines" of protectorate administrations. His home, then his school — Christian elementary, Christian high school, and finally Christian college — all have reinforced for him the nature of the culture that hangs upon the premise of survival on the basis of isolation and insulation from the world, which is done by "finding a ministry."

To the C.I., the Christian business organization is one more step in the "gravitational pull" of the institution. For him this is no "call" necessarily, but a natural flow of his life from the cradle to the grave. More than that, he comes into the organization as one conditioned for the familiar patterns of Christian institutional culture. Though he does not admit it to himself, he has come to depend on that pattern for his own survival. He knows nothing else. He has not been exposed to the option of making his way in the world. The world, especially as a possible place for making a living, is almost a terrifying fate if he should in any way fail in his "Christian service." He knows nothing of its style, relationships, or conduct and has come to view it early in life as "the last possible option."

To C.I., the Christian organization, does, in fact, become "redemptive." It saves him from the world, the entanglement with it, and the trauma of seeking to negotiate his way through a jungle of "spiritual traps" that could in the end destroy him. In this sense, he will tolerate the stresses and strains of the organization's "spiritual retreat syndrome," knowing well the nature of the Alexander Simons. He will accommodate easily to the illogical systems, the superimposed proscriptions, the consequent helter-skelter work flow. He does so because he has learned to accommodate to these throughout his life within the controlled Christian institution that has dominated him. He has learned to revere the "God figure" as authoritarian who in that role possesses all that C.I. could possibly own as an individual endowed by God. Erich Fromm's analysis of this yielding to the authoritarian God principle is that "this man projects his most valuable powers unto God [or the God figure] ... and his own powers then have become separated from him, and in this process he has become alienated from himself. Everything he has now is God's" — and now is projected to Alexander Simon — "and nothing is left in him. His only access to himself is through God [or the God figure]. In worshiping God he tries to get in touch with that part of himself which he has lost through projection. After having given God all he has, he begs God to return to him some of what originally was his own."

The point has already been alluded to that God does not seek to throttle His own in that fashion. But C.I. has already learned the credo of "no rights, no questions, no complaints," which are all part of a "proper spiritual demeanor toward all images of authority." Simon has become the embodiment of all those images of his past, the parent image, pastor image, professor image, camp director image, school president image, etc. To resist them is to resist God. To even suggest a "better way" constitutes the same level of dereliction.

Therefore, C.I. will ride with the "tide of events," knowing it to be a less traumatic route.

The fact that forty-six of the seventy-eight people in *Simon's Signposts* are Christian Conditioned Institutionals substantiates Simon's own concept of them. For him, the C.I. is a reinforcement of his own organizational concepts. The C.I. is "dedicated and committed" not only to God, but to Simon. Which means Simon will have less complaint from them, less resistance, and therefore they compose less of a threat to the "well-being and smooth-flowing operation" of the company. In this, he is in most instances correct.

But in making his conclusions about the C.I., he also underestimates the real inner longings of these individuals as a whole. For while they will bow to his dictates, on the surface at least, while they do not seek in any sense to pose a threat or even cultivate images of resistance, they nevertheless have urgent needs for their own lives that they seek to have met in the organization.

The C.I., having had the one-dimensional institutional "watch-care" all of his life, has come into *Simon's Signposts* in search of the "holy grail" as it were — it is in essence the need for new challenges, a desire to know himself in the test of manhood or womanhood which has been denied in the circumspect behavioral patterns of early institutional training. The C.I. wants mountains to climb, tunnels to build, oceans to cross. At least he wants to find that level which is solely entrusted to him as his "responsibility," to "make the crooked places straight" and thus to prove to himself that as a Christian God wants him to face life. That will come with the source of motivation and joy.

In a real sense, the C.I. poses a peculiar dilemma; he is, as Fromm puts it, as all men, "a herd animal. His actions are determined by an instinctive impulse to follow the leader and to have close contact with the other animals around him. Inasmuch as we are sheep, there is no greater threat to our existence than to lose this contact with the herd and to be isolated... but the split between our sheep-nature and our human-nature is the basis of two kinds of orientations: the orientation by proximity to the herd and the orientation by reason...."

The C.I. is caught in the "expression of a basic

dichotomy in man, the coextensive need for bondage and freedom. . . ."

For C.I., then, the failure to attain the level of freedom to think as a rational being, to be given responsible tasks that allow for a measure of personal contribution to the effecting of them, will lead him finally to a crippling inferiority complex. Then he will attempt to find solace in the spiritual motions of the herd that will subdue the urges within.

But, as Fromm says, "The more he praises God, the emptier he becomes. The emptier he becomes, the more sinful he feels. The more sinful he feels, the more he praises God — and the less able he is to regain himself."

In the end he will become even more hypercritical of the organizational management than those who come into the organization from the business world. But in that he faces a threat. He cannot make his criticisms known to the proper authority figures on top, for fear that it might get back to Simon. That would mean he "would be found out as one who is resisting the God-anointed authority." The C.I. does not want to be known as a "resister or complainer" lest he be tagged as faithless or not fit to be a part of the Christian organization. That could mean loss of face or even dismissal. To be dismissed or "counseled to consider what God has in mind" would mean another organization of the same impasses. Or else it would force him to turn to that "other world" which holds only the spectres of unholy enterprise.

He is confined, then, to taking his grievances out on the lower echelon of his peer group within the organization who suffer the same paralysis as he. They, like himself, are unable by the nature of their task and departmental proximity to Simon, as listed on the "organizational chart" — if there is one — to find the channels through which they can share their urge to contribute, to suggest a "better way." Immediate supervisors are locked into the same binds, for they dare not carry the longings or feelings of the "oppressed" upward lest Simon conclude that they are "failing in their spiritual responsibility to still the spirit of complaint."

The C.I., in essence, is not asking much. His complaints are not geared to lead to the storming of the head office. What he has come to expect is within the trust placed upon Alexander Simon by God Himself, simply the matter of "making productive people out of what they can do" and even long to do.

In the end, the Christian Conditioned Institutional organization man is to be sympathized with: He has no reprieve. He has nowhere to go. He is locked into the one-dimensional "spiritual" mantle fitted to him years before, which has become a pinching suit of armor preventing him from any kind of mobility. If he resents having been fit at all, it is understandable. He will go on carping and complaining in the shipping room but "smiling" and "rejoicing" in the throne room. His near schizophrenic posture will affect his spiritual balance. But if he can draw on the spiritual rationales for his "state" long enough, there may come a time when he no longer responds to his "urges" to climb mountains, cross oceans, or "solve a major problem facing the company." At that point he will become docile, accommodating, functional, and "model." His "spirit of complaint" will cease, but the fires of his heart will also have gone out.

His struggle, then, is to fight that pull to docility and to keep hope alive. He will fight the oversimplified spiritual solution or the "language that is supposed to alter the complexity of the problem." He will count his paper clips, shuffle his papers, perform his mere "functions" to which he is assigned — always entertaining the hope that "things will get better."

2. *The Christian Executive Type*

The Christian Executive type refers to the man or woman who comes into the Christian organization already having proved themselves in the secular business world. Some have been Christians a long time; some, like Pearl Munson, only a few years. The distinction is not in their years in the faith so much as in the expertise they bring into the company, and more particularly the "dreams" they entertain as being fulfilled in "God's work."

The C.E. comes into the organization almost completely naive as to the "state of the union" that is *Simon's Signposts*. In some cases, depending on his years and exposure to the church operation, he will have some inkling that there is a kind of "loose federation" with a lot of tag ends and continual spinning off of either people or paper. He senses inwardly that he is entering an arena that is limited in its skills since these are subsidiary to the "ideological demands." He knows intuitively that there must be some malfunction, some levels of mediocrity and substandard operational guidelines. These, he concludes, are challenges for him.

However, this is not that to which he is "called." Alexander Simon, in recruiting the C.E., does not ever refer to organizational problems. His "challenge" is to the fact that *"Signposts* is at a point where it can go no other direction but up — I want you to come and join us, brother, and soar with the rest of us. Let God have your talents, bury them with Him, and I assure you a blessing you won't be able to contain." Such a "call" is hard to turn aside. Nevertheless, the C.E. does not rush blindly into the "rapture" either. Schooled by years of caution in secular business, he will wait. But sensing the "strong pull to allow God to have the benefit of what I've learned," the C.E. does come to that moment of truth. His disciplines force reality into his response — he is going to "help that organization achieve its goals, God helping me." But he has to admit at the same time that "the attractiveness is there, to be able to give my energies in an atmosphere of mutual understanding and collective decision making as opposed to the dog-eat-dog relationships too often experienced in secular business."

The motives may not be 100 percent pure, but the expectations, as categorically described by Simon, are properly based. Christian work should and ought to be exactly that, a place where, even if order is missing, at least there is a sense of relaxed confidence in each other to construct the order together. The Christian organization, as no other, begs the characteristics of purpose, peace, collective decision making, and opportunity to work hard in an atmosphere of mutual respect and cooperation. (And there are those who have arrived.)

The C.E. type has every right to expect that he is crossing over from a jungle-like complexity of secular value systems into a "true vineyard principle" where honesty, integrity, respect, and the value of the individual take precedence. He knows business must be business, but he believes, in all of that, that he can still know the illusive ingredients of love, understanding, and unselfish concern.

The C.E. has come to believe, looking from the outside, that any organization that could come to a $1,000,000 profit picture in a few years must have the ideals of organizational know-how and godly character running through it. He realizes that God does not bestow these automatically, but they must be worked at; and Simon must have done a lot of "working at it." He does not know, however, that the president has risen to the head of a successful company despite his own limitations, and that he is quick and vocal in reminding the world and the church of that. C.E. has no idea that the company is *not* successful in the terms he thinks, but in the measure of what he fought as *success* in secular business — money.

If he had known, would his "calling" have changed? Probably not. God saw it all and knew that *Signposts* needed "business sense" lest it blow apart. Mercifully, He hid the glaring gaps in the organizational make-up and sent C.E. in on the basis of his "ideals." Who hasn't followed that star and come to the moment of truth? And yet, was it a mistake to go? No. As God sends a man with "high ideals" into a "grimly real problem," He likewise hopes with the man that the "seeding" of such commitment will have some bearing upon the shape of the structure and the president.

But the "structure" is still Simon. And if the C.E. is not going to fulfill his "ideals" about his own contribution to the company, it is tied up finally in Simon's own view of the executive type as being "more or less a necessary strategy." Simon would much prefer that his "executive rank" be staffed by the "full-time, fully committed, fully familiar" institutionally conditioned Christian type. But he has to admit that his growing company needs the kind of "executive supervision" and know-how that will keep things in line." That last statement, which is a left-handed job description, would have posed an interesting reaction in the Christian Executive if he had been informed that this, in effect, was to be his responsibility.

What it says is that Simon was not hiring executives for new ideas or even contributions on how to run the company. He was, in essence, hiring them as "supervisors" of a work pattern already established by himself. Simon, at the same time, is never too comfortable in hiring any executive who carries "years of experience and insight into the complexities of business." Such a person could, in fact, overshadow Simon himself and pose "some serious internal imbalances," which means "such a person could bump rather rudely into the God figure pillars and contradict rightful control." The fact that Simon would rather staff, and does so, on the basis of weakness rather than strength is indicative of his inner fear of getting too strong a man in a sensitive area of his company. Simon, sensing his limitations in corporate structure, knows that he could be found out if he should get a man who is "not spiritually right for the job."

Which means, a man who sees too clearly and expresses himself too boldly and acts too decisively.

What Simon should have seen was that his "executive staff" — especially the C.E. type — could be his "salvation." There is one critical contribution the C.E. can bring into a Christian company which Simon needed desperately. As Drucker says in his book, the "effective executive tries to make fully productive the strengths of his own superior." Or, as he adds, "the effective executive makes the strengths of his boss productive."

The C.E. has learned this kind of relationship in his secular business. He feels it is his responsibility to help his president come to the full productive power that is his, though buried deep within the spiritual gloss. The C.E. does that, because in so doing, his own position and his own strengths become more productive. But the initiative for this must come from Simon, and that will demand a capacity to listen. And Simon is not a listener. For him, control is contingent upon "his ability to command the agenda, the conversation, to steer it, guide it, and lead it to where he feels the executive must finally come."

This is contrary to Antony Jay's *Corporation Man,* when he says, "The willingness to listen first and decide afterward has sorted out the successful leaders from the unsuccessful."

As it is, then, the C.E. is hardly settled in his office before he comes to realize that he is not to "make decisions regarding his department in any area, but that his suggestions must be weighed collectively with other vice-presidents." What that means, finally, is that it will be "weighed by the president himself." To come into an organization with abilities and knowledge in decision making, initiative, and creative function and then be put down into a mere "departmental prop" is the first solid shock wave to his "idealism." What is to be so frustrating to the C.E. is that "he is let down so nicely by Simon who does it all in the name of the Lord."

From then on, the C.E.'s problems will spin completely around that dictate.

What will become even more frustrating, and lean heavily on him with the press of futility, will not be the spiritual overlay that hangs so heavy, but rather how to dig out from that the necessary business policies needed to guarantee work flow and production.

What will nag him day and night is to know which end of the spiritual-business or business-spiritual he is to employ to explain the lack of promotion, wages, and advancements within his own department. For the dictate is "to make certain his people are spiritually oriented to the task."

But to him there is no such thing as "spiritual orientation to a physical task." There can only be challenges to concentration, "skill development" for tasks, and proper incentives. He can allow for a "spiritual attitude" toward the task, but that's as far as he can actually go. But since there has been no real "task orientation" in any sense, and people continually operate out of line with their skills or aptitudes, there is really nothing left but to appeal to their "spiritual orientation," if for nothing else than to keep them from losing all perspective.

Now it will be up to him to fight the other end of the spectrum, when the "business side" demands of him the "fast shuffle" to "improve the sales image." It will be up to him to run the line that separates integrity from questionable ethics. It will be up to him to learn to "wink the eye" at the close corners cut across the shape of morality in business — certainly Christian business — and to own up to the failure in the "spiritual sense" as "simply something you have to do to win a proper place for God in the marketplace."

In all of this, Simon has learned to use his "executive staff" as a buffer against all these contradictory principles as well as a barrier to the rank and file. Where Simon has not the ability nor the taste for trying to balance the business and spiritual dimensions, he will shift it to his vice-presidents who have actually come into the company "to learn that from him."

Finally, it will be C.E. burning the midnight oil, not so much in actual work, but rather trying to sort out in his mind where all this has taken him and if maybe the "call of God" was misplaced. In the end, he will either have to experience some detachment from his "ideals" and learn to shift with the "practical demands of a hopelessly confused maze of organizational malfunction" or remove himself from it entirely.

So why does he stay? Unlike the C.I. who has nowhere to go, the Christian Executive can still return to his old job in secular business. There he would be welcomed with open arms, recognized for his expertise, knowledge, and decision making power. But it is not quite that simple.

The C.E. has burned his bridges, made his vows to God, committed himself "by life or by death" to "Christian work." He has declared it to his church, his business friends, his neighbors. To go back now would be an admission of failure. For himself, he wouldn't mind. But in the withdrawal, the failure would be charged to God, or to the failure of the Christian organization to absorb the talents of the business mind. In any case, for the Christian Executive, retreat demands painful explanations. To him, that compromises the image of God. So he stays.

He could make a horizontal shift to another Christian organization, always hoping that he will find that "ideal." If he keeps moving often enough, he has the possibility of making that connection. But how many moves can an executive afford before his "credential file" becomes suspect?

So he stays. He learns to detach himself from the plaguing doubts and the daily mash of "hop, skip, and jump" work patterns. He will learn to "adjust" to those demands of "building the product image," on the premise that "we are after all a business." He will learn to accommodate himself to the impossibility of "telling" anything of his concerns to the president or ever attempting to "share" fully his own dilemmas about his place and role in the company. He will learn the right "spiritual language" that has the "certain sound" which says "all things are in proper perspective," which is to say, "this is a ministry regardless of the profits, sales, and advertising budgets."

If he continues on that route, he may learn to "settle down" and "make the best of it." But there will be times even then when he will ask himself if he is paying more by staying rather than leaving.

When asked one of those open-ended questions about organizational policy, purpose, or aims, he will be able to say, "I just work here." When he has arrived at that point, his "calling" will have become simply a job.

3. *The Christian Institutional Executive*

There is another type of executive who should be mentioned here. He is the Christian Institutional Executive, better known as C.I.E. He has not been groomed by secular business experience. He has been a Christian a long time, maybe not from childhood, but long enough to "sense the system of things." The C.I.E. is out to "make the best of it" and sees the Christian organization as the one means to attaining and holding some level of executive rank with its attendant "status." He has won his way into that position mostly by "loyalty and faithfulness" to Simon. He has learned to make the system work for him by "not rocking the boat." He senses anyway, and probably correctly, that he will know no other heights in his "career" except those which Simon will measure for him. He knows his limitations, but he also knows that the strengths in the area of expertise and know-how, such as C.E. carries, do not command that much influence with Simon. So he will practice at the "devotional levels" of the operation, in keeping with

Simon's "sense of priority." The business side, to him, will "get done somehow." He is not necessarily happy with the role he has learned to play, but he is, after all, "a realist." He has learned to swing with Simon's moods, temperament, and "expectant wishes" and thus avoids any kind of confrontation that could put him on shaky ground.

In between C.I., C.E., and C.I.E. lies that middle ground occupied by people who don't fit totally in any of these dimensions. Many of them are not institutionally conditioned nor secularly wise in business but nevertheless fully expect some kind of "promised land" fulfillment. Many of them don't know who they really are with respect to the organization, where they fit in, or what they really ought to expect. For most of them it, too, "is a job." Some of them had to come to terms long ago with "the system of things," like C.I.E. In so doing, they have found some level of contentment, not particularly concerned with straining after something, they know not what. For others, who know they cannot change things anyway, it boils down to "putting in our time and hoping it comes out all right."

The mesh of all these counterforces and neutral forces in the organization is not so much different from the secular structure. Except, however, that in the secular there is usually a strong managing center that keeps the imbalances and personality clashes in check. Executive management in secular operations is hired and paid on its ability to work with these corporate distinctives and keep the lines clear between executives and rank and file. Top management in secular firms puts great emphasis on keeping junior and department executives conscious of task and performance levels and the rewards attendant to them. Thus, with all energies focused on the one area of concern, and conscious of this strong and infusing management on top, the work force has little time or less inclination to wrangle over the subsurface problems of tangled motivations and philosophies.

In the Christian organization, on the other hand, and again there are exceptions, there is no strong "top management" as such. The center of the "corporation" functions purely on the spiritual interpretation of principles governing task and people. Everything is boiled down to "spiritual attitude," regardless of the problem and the solutions submitted. The executives are left with the problems of settling tensions within their own cadre, "since spiritually mature people are expected to settle such petty differences anyway." Simon does not see the potential dangers of the cross-purpose work philosophies of C.E. who is dedicated to performance proficiency, C.I.E. who is content with whatever is, or C.I. who is constantly pushing "to find himself in meaningful responsibility."

To ignore the warning signs, however, is to court disaster. As Antony Jay puts it: "Two of the major disqualifications for a leader are to be deaf to the warning signals from the pack and to fail to learn from experience."

Meanwhile, the tensions will continue to grow, creeping relentlessly in the subsurface nerve channels of the organization. They are never openly articulated but only "lived with," because to air them is "not the spiritual thing to do." When they finally erupt, a prized C.E. will resign to escape the pressure. Simon will get the word and, in the style of his credo, will say, "Well, if that's the way the Lord is leading you, sorry as I am, that's it. . . ." And out the door will go five years, or even more, of experience and investment with hardly a feeble gasp of protest.

To rise to that particular kind of mix in management levels — to say nothing of the rank and file — is almost impossible without sensitive leadership, fully aware of the complexity and ultimate destruetiveness of it.

And yet, even with this complexity of people at cross-purpose, with the attendant frustrations moving all down the line, the sense of imbalance and tension might be held at bay if just one "ideal" was somehow satisfied in the daily cleaving to "functionality." For all corporations, or even smaller units of business-ministry, find that the rank and file will always manage to stick at it if they can find that illusive "sense of belonging."

Almost everyone in Christian organizations, regardless of their activities or rank, confess a deep-seated need "to belong." It is in the nature of the Christian enterprise, as in no other, to provide that by its unique composition linked with its "sense of cause." For one thing, it poses an image that is intrinsically "family," bringing people together who hold to similar views and passions, bound together by the "solidarities" of the faith. It is almost "sibling," or should be, in its interpersonal relationships, merging diverse personalities and skills into a common purpose. The organization goes beyond product in its inner wealth. It is, in the very nature of its being, one with God. The people drawn to it, then, are those who have come to expect a "meaningful tie," like branches being grafted onto a tree.

And yet it seems so few find this "sense of belonging," even though God certainly must long that they experience it. Too many are merely "passing through" and have no intention of commitment to any given length of time. Why they don't find a sense of belonging is tied to the same problem that is Alexander Simon's in his organizational ethos — that the attributes of God do not automatically manifest themselves "where two or three are gathered together." They must be infused, developed, and nurtured by precept and certainly by example.

Antony Jay states, in his comment on the corporation: "As long as everyone in the corporation understands what the whole job is, where the tribe is going, where he fits into it, and what everyone else is up to, and as long as there is a rich, informal network with people thinking with or ahead of each other and confident of each other's loyalty, then there are safety nets at every point. Without this sort of community, you have to fall back on authority. . . ."

When there is an interlocking of people within a Christian organization, coming out of a respect for the gifts each brings into the group — and the limitations as well; when there is recognition of each other as being an invaluable part to each other and then to the end product, but not before; when there is a sense of collective and personal triumph each day in the fact of confronting men with that "product" which God will bless because the people who are producing it are "blessed," there is the beginning of a genuine sense of belonging.

If leadership will take the time to define that and demonstrate it, the rank and file will be quick to cultivate it — or at least they should. Perhaps not everyone in the Christian organization is going to find his or her fulfillment to the fullest extent of his "ideal," in that "sense of belonging." But where there runs through the mainstream of the organization the interlocking spirit of people looking for the highest good in each other, each individual will come to some level upon which he can stand.

To get a man from the empty "I only work here" commentary to the statement of commitment that says "I belong here" is not that big a gap to bridge. It ought to begin with trust, a trust that shows itself on the part of the leader in allowing responsibility or opportunity to create, experiment, and even make mistakes. Trust is cardinal to organizational value. It is a trust born out of a sense of realization that the people sent into the organization are "God sent," regardless of whether the people themselves sense that entirely. It is trust that should be demonstrated by the leader in his willingness to "expose" himself in genuine informal identification with his rank and file, without feeling that it will cancel his sense of "godly authority." A pat on the shoulder, a word of encouragement, even giving a man a job bigger than his capacity, can be the beginning of that emergent "sense of belongingness."

In the end, though, Simon could thank God for those

whom he considers "expendable" elements in the final balance of things. The fact that they stick, in spite of the frustrated expectations and fractured dreams; the fact that they hang on to the flimsy hopes that so often burn down; the fact that, in spite of it all, they will defend their organization and, oddly enough, even Alexander Simon proves something of the stuff of which they are made. In the defending of Simon, it demonstrates how much the organizational man feels Simon to be an extension of himself — it proves that the ingredients of cohesion are there, that the "ten group" is struggling to emerge. Often their loyalties will remain fierce when hard-pressed, simply because they see the organization as "God's little acre" and somehow they have a piece of that custodianship.

On this, indeed, does the Kingdom of God advance!

But, meanwhile, C.I., C.E., and C.I.E. — and all those in between — must negotiate their "maze"; hope must, after all, come second to reality, and reality is the ever-present present. The exasperations of a single day will mount. They know that exasperations are everyone's lot, but because of the peculiar ones which arise out of the sacrosanct arena of spiritual enterprise, they will always wonder, "Is this exasperation really necessary?"

On that does the "state of the union" rest with considerable discomfort.

V

The Status Complex – Up the Down Staircase?

How then do the giant misplaced steps of organizational ethos in leadership and executive effectiveness, or the lack of it, finally begin to show up in the fallout?

Simon's concepts of goals, values, tasks, strengths, and his presumptions regarding his employees' need for a "sense of belonging" as already deposited in them by God, have all been cast through a spiritual filter in keeping with his intent to be the "spiritual father" in a complex corporational system.

He fell short in his organizational aims and goals to begin with because of his insistence on applying the spiritual credo to the mundane demands. Some matters of business will simply not roll over for the spiritual application. This does not say that the spiritual is not important. What it says is that there is a complex duality — a ministry *and* a business — and each demands its specific inputs and controls, even values. Simon's refusal — or maybe even inability — to see the business as distinct in its basic demands from the spiritual and vice versa grew out of his own sense of limitation in corporation or business affairs that applied to a growing company. Beyond that, of course, as was noted, all of it stemmed, in large measure at least, from his life style credo that resulted in the stance of a spiritual authoritarian locked into the principle of total obedience as a proper fulfillment of Jesus' "vineyard principle" (Matthew 20:1-16). Yet none of this had to spell disaster. Limitations can be overcome. At any given point in the history of the company Simon could have evaluated himself in terms of his people and seen it all. And yet did he expect it all to be worked out by someone else? Did his "garage syndrome" prevent that kind of self-examination?

It must be said at this point that the problems directly spawned by the Simons are not necessarily different in terms of the size of the organization. Naturally, the larger the business — ministry or corporation — the less will be felt of the leader's direct influence. The larger the corporation, the more responsibility is placed on department executives to discharge goals and values. The smaller the business, the more directly will the influence of the top be felt.

But large or small, all of the matters of direction, ethos, and value are modified finally by the titular head. Everyone must inevitably come to terms with the atmosphere of control as set at the top. There is no way for executives to operate independently of that influence. Some try for the sake of their own departmental personnel, but in the end, that which is not in line with the top man comes into collision.

Because the Christian organization is bound together in its personality mesh by the nature of its emergence under God, it does not allow for independent attitudes in departmental procedures. The word travels fast — too fast. A spirit of laxity or freedom given in one department is soon picked up by those not so equally attended.

The result is a confrontation with the "big man" who will not tolerate "departures" from policy, even though very little policy is ever really articulated.

The point here, then, is that the larger the corporation, the more responsibility the president has to communicate to his executive staff and to allow them more freedom to set the pace of performance and norms. The smaller the organization, the more the president must move among his rank and file, making his presence a guide upon which to draw a proper fix.

Alexander Simon's company is caught between smallness and largeness, and in this state of neither-nor it is imperative that his authoritarian grip be relaxed some to permit breathing room. His view, however, is that growth demands tighter control to make certain "no one gets out of line."

The effects of this one-dimensional approach on the complex business of merging diverse personalities and expertise has been noted in part already. But the totality of it has yet to emerge in what are considered the "critical test points" of organizational or corporation success. Again, success is used here in terms of the attitude of the people who comprise it and not in the profit and loss statement. It is in this "test point" area that an employee is either going to suffer trauma and ultimately take on that "complex" about himself and his job, or rise to new levels of understanding of himself with the accompanying higher motivations to the task.

One of the "critical test points" ignored almost completely at *Simon's Signposts* is the matter of *status*. To Simon, status is what a man gets when he becomes a Christian, that is, being a child of God, "an heir with Him." Beyond that, awarding of status to any individual is akin to bowing to "worldly postures and the world's measurement of worth." In the strictly spiritual sense, he is correct. The child of God, while remaining within the context of the spiritual mystique, has already been given equality to his brother by virtue of the atonement; he need not resort to "status symbols" to declare his place in the Kingdom of God.

On the other hand, when shifting over to the more mundane matters of the business organization, where roles are determined in terms of task — or ought to be — "status" is necessary for two reasons: one, it gives the worker an awareness of the significance of his performance in relationship to others and provides incentives; second, it gives him the necessary credential, if he has that kind of position, to reinforce his authority in decision making toward others. Status, then, is a device for developing the necessary authority figures (not authoritarian) and assures a proper flow of communication from the right source. This, in turn, builds order and cohesion.

1. *Status — The Position*

Simon, if he considers status as even legitimate in the spiritual sense, will seek to define it in the titles he gives. The longer the title, the greater the status, as he sees it. Some of this gets to be quite bizarre: Department of Consumer Analysis and Product Control sounds very impressive, but all it refers to is the Sales Department; Supervisor of Product Image and Market Differential Analysis is simply the complicated, though grandiose, description for the Promotion Department; Director of Content Development and Visual Data Profiling and Projection is the five-mile verbal journey for what is simply the Editor; or Director of Compartment Traffic, Pattern, Flow, and Surveillance is quite a laugh when it really means Captain of Security.

It may be fun — until someone has to introduce someone else in one of those departments. "Then the eyeballs start rolling and the smoke comes out of the ears," said one employee. "But you've got to hand it to Simon; when you throw out one of those ten-foot titles at your local banker, he actually looks like he wants to ask *you* for a loan!"

Nevertheless, the fact remains, titles without authority and certainly without the pay do little to impress the herd. Vice-presidents who are still licking stamps in their departments, for lack of personnel, have hardly arrived at any sense of status that will give credence to their command. Department heads who must take their turn at preparing coffee for the coffee break — because "nothing is too menial for the servant of God," as Simon puts it — have long since lost any "status" that might have been intended with the title.

Status, then, should be given by the director either on the basis of the paycheck or by the position in direct proximity to the top management, which is himself. The normal fixing of it is in terms of both pay and position. Unfortunately, *Simon's Signposts* comes last in both considerations.

But to Simon's credit, and after seven years of reading or "dipping through" the business magazines, a "sudden click" resounded in the cleanly swept corridors of his brain. Now that his company was growing, so the magazine said, it was time for an organizational chart to "determine the ranking of departments to each other and finally to top management." It may have been a little after the fact now, with the company already running on its in-built system of helter-skelter task orientation, but there is never a point beyond which a man cannot begin to set his house in order. The chart could, if properly handled, have helped his executive staff who needed some clarification of their own status, if for no other reason than to get some strength for command and help them properly relate to each other.

However, Simon, by his penchant to reinforce his own command, built his chart showing how everyone — the total rank and file — was to relate to *himself*. Rather than making it show "status" in terms of interdepartmental authority relationships, it was to reinforce his own "status of command."

Further, his insistence on drawing up a total organizational rank and file chart and showing it to everyone at Tuesday morning's devotional time was to drastically reverse the "good intention" of it. To draw up a chart to show the relationship of his executives to each other and to him was one thing, and much needed. But to superficially, at best, construct such a design for the entire work force was but to compound the already complicated role-playing of each of them.

The value of organizational charts in this sense has been the object of debate in corporation structure anyway. Antony Jay says of it, "The organization chart causes more exasperation than any other piece of paper; it is drawn up in good faith by men who are trying to deploy the corporation staff effectively for success [not quite Simon's purpose] in the survival battle. But everyone is looking at it as evidence of how the corporation finally judges his status."

Simon's third problem with that chart was in the design of it. Since it was drawn up primarily to show everyone where he stood in relationship to Simon, it was a purely vertical structure. On top was the huge square marked "president." Down from that extended a line of boxes, stacked in horizontal rows looking like birdhouses, diminishing in size until it ended in the last tiny blob, hardly discernible, marked "custodian."

Now it was perfectly clear how "status" could be determined by anyone in the company. All he had to do was measure the size of the "box" that was his in comparison with either the president's "control tower" or the broom closet at the other end. Billy Rawlson, the custodian, was to be known thereafter as the "lower end of Simon's continuum" whose "status" was as significant as the lonely gravedigger's. For him, looking toward the top was like staring up through a long pipe, the other end of which got smaller and smaller until no light could be seen at all.

In any case, more than 60 percent of the working force got the message that day, since they fell below the line which appeared to be anywhere near "the sun." Their "status," then, in the mind of the organization "brain," was clearly spelled out, whether he intended it to come off in those exact stratification dimensions or not. For them, viewing the array of birdhouse boxes above them, the journey to the top or anywhere near it would be like running a major obstacle course. Without any recognized status on the chart to begin with, in terms of authority lines, these people would sense total futility in knowing, what they had refused to accept up to now, that they were the "expendables of the expendables."

This was unfortunate, because many of the jobs in that "lower broom closet stratification" were critical to the total production. And that also included the custodian. But as it stood, the chart served no useful purpose; in fact, it brought out a new "sense of complex" to the many productive units in the company. And with that would come new tensions. Since most of them were already working for a reduced pay scale, to be relegated to almost the "least" in terms of contribution was to be an extremely heavy extra burden to bear.

Actually, if Simon had taken one more crucial step and made that chart into a "mobility flow," showing the avenues by which the work force could move upward in terms of task and status, it could have been a valuable guide and even an incentive builder. Then the fixed positions in the "birdhouse chart" would not have appeared so final and so demeaning.

Was it a lack of intelligence on Simon's part that he failed to see that? Not necessarily. What it demonstrates again is the rather spasmodic impulses of a man willing to take the "risk" on possible repercussions to the chart, knowing or assuming that the "ministry" of the organization presumed a great deal of tolerance and forbearance on the part of the rank and file. But when an individual's livelihood is at stake, when people are struggling to better themselves and improve their living, they have less inclination to be played with. Their sense of tolerance as Christians will always be there of course — but there is a line across which it will not be pushed. Simon simply failed to know where that line was.

It is not a question, then, of dropping the "status" principle just because the president couldn't define it aptly enough to get the needed result. In secular business, of course, there is greater emphasis given to it than in the Christian organization. In that arena, it is incumbent on the administration to declare the status badges in order to hold the right people in the critical jobs.

In a Christian organization, however, the nature of the organism is different, so declaration of status has to be different. Even the design of it must be tailored to the organizational relationships intrinsic to it. It should be somewhat in keeping with the "vineyard principle" that Jesus taught in His parable about wages, referred to earlier (Matthew 20:1-16). In that instance it was not a lesson on the insignificance of wages, but more a positive declaration of a value in such relationships that goes beyond money. It teaches that "status" in the working force must be determined in keeping with the "family grouping" and not only or even simply as productive units.

One Christian organization designed such a chart in a circular format. The circle was to represent the "decision making core" which included the president and the three vice-presidents. Around that circle were grouped the departments, each one touching on that circle. This design clearly indicated that each department and the people working in it had equal access to the circle and equal opportunity. The circle concept demonstrated the nature of the binding relationships of a Christian organization rather than the vertical "class structure" that Simon designed. The circle put no one down into the depths and therefore avoided the unfortunate impression that some in the Kingdom of God were, indeed, last.

2. Status — The Task

If a Christian worker cannot find an awareness of his status in his positional fix with the company, and he has not yet sensed it in his pay, then he will certainly look for it in the *task* entrusted to him.

Someone has said that the last level of pride for the worker in any organization is the job he does. It is no different in a Christian enterprise.

The confusion with regard to task orientation in *Simon's Signposts* has already been established. The absence of any clear-cut job description is intentional perhaps, since Simon feels that "once a man is pegged into a single job, he loses his responsibility to be ready for anything. The Body demands flexibility."

But the Body, even in the spiritual sense that he uses it, does not function on *duplicated* efforts. "Flexibility" does not mean the hand also doing the work of the foot and vice versa, and yet that is exactly what occurs in the job program at *Signposts*. There is that constant sense of people shuffling in and out of each other's particular "domain," each having some little bit of some job. It is not surprising then that the "task proficiency" is very low and employees feel that lack of commitment to task which is so vital to status.

Simon further rationalizes his "open-ended" job assignments on the basis that to peg specific jobs for individuals would "mean having to double the work force. With everyone willing to pitch in where he can, you see, we can keep our personnel down and still get the job done."

On the contrary, corporation management has already proven that when jobs are intelligently blocked out and specifically defined, and when people are found who have the talents to perform them, the work force can actually be cut. Task proficiency comes when the worker knows fully what is expected of him in what he is doing. Experience in that task brings him to a high level of productivity; as his level goes up, so does his morale. And with it comes his sense of "status," which is the pride in accomplishing something vital. When that is recognized in the "status stratification" of the company, his proficiency jumps even more and the need for extra help often is not necessary.

Before Pearl Munson came into *Signposts* and insisted on "job descriptions" and a closer monitoring of "task orientation," Simon's "open-endedness in job placement" created a fantastic dimension of "happy insanity." What was happening was that a man or woman accepted for a "general job situation" within the "general area of promotion and advertising" sometimes would never get there. Somewhere along the line he or she would be intersected by some hard-pressed department head who was hurting for staff and "put to work." The phrase "Simon's raiders" was to describe the activities of those department heads who would often solicit personnel from other work situations or else "lay their hands suddenly" on some unsuspecting new recruits and put them to work regardless of what their qualifications were.

All of this was in keeping, of course, with the company's "policy" of "doing all things in Christ." It was but a step up or over from the "general missionary" syndrome, but what it did to "task proficiency" and "status" is obvious.

Case History 1

Alice W. Wonderland came to *Simon's Signposts* after eighteen years as an executive secretary for a department store manager. Her credentials were in the area of statistical secretary, and she had answered *Signpost's* ad for a "detail secretary, good at typing and with numbers." She could type ninety words a minute, was a whiz as a steno, and had a mind for detail. She was a shy, petite, almost fragile blonde, just pushing forty.

Alice was "assigned" to the promotion-advertising department who had placed the ad. But Alice never did get to the typewriter, nor to the department. A junior executive in charge of sales whipped her off into a spacious, cold, barren office at the far end of the building which had a single wooden desk, a couple of file cabinets, and a huge painting of John the Baptist baptizing Jesus in the Jordan. She was given a chair for the desk and five manila folders loaded with back correspondence from hotels and convention centers asking if *Simon's Signposts* intended to take exhibit space for the following year.

Alice W. Wonderland was to become the "Supervisor of Sales Conventions," but she wasn't told that until two months later. In those two months she simply tried to find her way through that correspondence and answer it. But from that she suddenly found herself booking those exhibit spaces in those convention centers and then seeing to the shipping of display material, supplies, etc. She didn't get too alarmed, however, until she was told she would attend those sales conventions. She had "osmoded" into a job for which nobody else seemed to have time.

For a full year Alice — quiet, reserved, fragile Alice — manned six of those sales conventions without complaint. What she did in that job was to get herself to the convention sites, put up six ten-foot wooden display boards, lift six twenty-five-pound arc lights into place above them, whip four eight-foot mahogany tables into the booth areas, and throughout the convention continually lift boxes of materials up to those tables for people to examine. On top of that she found herself having to "public relate" and "sell" Simon's bumper stickers to would-be customers. Though other male personnel from Simon's sales force would drop by now and then "to see how things were," their primary task was to take clients for coffee breaks and lunches.

What Alice W. Wonderland actually gained that year was not that sense of "status" that should go with her natural talents as a whiz "statistical" secretary. What she did get was an unseemly set of biceps and, as a result of her miserable attempts to "public relate" out of a nonpublic relations aptitude and proficiency, a "monstrous complex" that landed her in the hospital with a nervous collapse. She would not come back to Simon's until she got her typewriter, which she finally did.

The company, however, hired a man for "sales conventions" who had come into the company originally as grounds keeper. He was not put into the job because he knew about sales conventions, but because he already had the biceps — where it all should have begun in the first place.

The case of Morton Hargrave's "incredible journey" has already been shown for the record and illustrates again what the "failure to find status in jobs" can do when it is ignored. Billy Rawlson's final stop in the "broom closet," after applying for "systems engineer," is another example.

A single day's routine of "job hopping" under this "open-ended" task orientation can bring the classic answer of one employee to a friend who had asked him what he did at Simon's. After a long pause, he said, "I forget."

The problem tied to the failure to articulate job descriptions and hold to them is compounded even further when too many hands insist on having some part of someone else's job.

Case History 2

Myron Downstreet, the "editor-in-chief in charge of copy and graphics," is a "key man" in the creative section of *Signposts*. On him rests the burden of coming up with the words and designs that will have impact on millions or "bomb out." Myron has been honored by various writing groups within the community of Christian artists for his "leadership in creative design and writing ingenuity." But only Myron, and a few sympathetic souls around him at Simon's, knows that he has never had one of his original ideas go straight from his desk to the print shop.

For in the "process of collective creativity" at Simon's every "idea" or "sketch" must go through four other departments for "approval" — sales, advertising, promotion, and cost analysis. Nobody knows why this has to be, and yet nobody stops to question it. It is one of those "policies." When each department has studied it and "made their changes," it goes to the next, eventually landing on Alexander Simon's desk for final clearance. There it either gets initialed as okay, or else it is "redone completely in keeping with our image." What comes back to the "creative director" is usually a four-dimensional monstrosity, approved by the president, which bears little resemblance to Myron Downstreet's original idea.

Needless to say, Myron does not want to talk about "status," and he may break into a fit of mad laughter if you ask him how his "job proficiency" is. At least he can laugh.

And if anyone asks him about the award for "graphic design and writing ingenuity," he will only stare at the floor.

How anything gets produced, shipped, and out to the "consumer" is often a point of deep pondering by those who dare to hazard such a mental search. For most of the people, it has to be "truly of God."

One male employee tried to explain it all this way: "One day we are a football team — all quarterbacks, however, each trying to get a piece of the ball and run with it.

"The next day we're like a hockey team with no skates, and brooms instead of sticks, trying to make a game of it in what is obviously a classic human comedy.

"And there are those real days when it's upset-the-fruit-basket, and we're all rushing into each other's departments as if we'd lost our wallets.

"And then there are those days when we can thank God for those eighteen closets in the place, because they are the only safe refuge left."

So they laugh about it. Thank God they will laugh! There is, nevertheless, a note of apology in that laugh, as if they are wishing for better things.

Meanwhile, they don't know much about "status" in their jobs. It obviously doesn't fit in a situation where no one knows for sure where his job begins or ends and which cannot be elevated to significance. And a work force, even in Christian work, that has lost that needed sense of value in the task, is bound to drift. And drift does not make for efficiency in production. Worse yet, it cuts deeply into morale.

If Simon realizes this problem, and in that realization sincerely wishes to face up to it and solve it, he can. A simple study of the "work flow," department by department, with his own executive staff and a few outside efficiency experts could reconstruct the organization in terms of task definition. From there, it would simply be a matter of reassignment of the people to the jobs outlined, assigning again from strengths, not from weaknesses. From there the matter of "status" would emerge, with people in their job roles grouped accordingly by department in terms of significance and performance.

Why he doesn't take that logical step is baffling to the best of analysts. But if it is to be traced to any one attitude or predisposition, it is simply that peculiar sense of accepting what is as *God-given, God-ordered,* and *God-maintained.* This near-fatalistic posture toward performance that says, "It will get done somehow, and it does get done in spite of us," hangs heavy over most of Christian work. To talk about "streamlining," "upgrading," or "updating" is to suggest that God is suspect in the "running of this business." To talk about "order and cohesion" is to negate God's already existent order, even though it may be a continual state of confusion, near chaos at times, and dissipating valuable energies. To suggest that there might "be a better way" to bring the talents and energies of the work force to their highest peak and thus assure better production and higher morale is to "tamper with God's own will with regard to how He will use His people and to what extent."

It could be, however, that Simon, already aware of his own lack of perception into the complexity of a growing business, may welcome the looseness of task orientation as being necessary for that "spirit of togetherness." The happy euphoria that is supposed to come with this kind of heavenly informality will bring them all to a realization of "feebleness, insufficiency, and dependency" on God that will in turn bring a new enablement "to do all things."

And "togetherness" in God's team is always the ideal, true, but it does not automatically guarantee performance. Only clear-cut task orientation plugged into that "togetherness" has the best possible assurance of success.

Or it could be, too, that Simon sees order, performance, proficiency, and systematizing as threats to the "spiritual ark" for which he has the custodianship under God. Such systematizing makes him fearful that the organization might get beyond his control. New systems of doing things — even though logically far better than what exists and promising far better production and work force morale — are viewed by Simon as meaning that he might be left behind in the "new order of things." What he does not realize is that these systems could win him far more respect and loyalty from his people, and in the end put him into a far more significant, contributing role than he now has.

The coming of Pearl Munson brought the first level of anything near stability and status in the job roles within *Simon's Signposts*. But even then Simon himself insisted on "flexibility" and often overruled the wisdom of his personnel director in favor of his own "God-given intuition about the people and the jobs." On these days the closets were full again.

So "it gets done" at *Signposts* — somehow, and the "Lord be praised." But perhaps the Lord would feel even more "thanked" if that sound was in unison all the way from the broom closet to the "control tower"; a united chorus of people who, at the end of the day, would genuinely praise Him for bringing them to the place where their specific strengths have been utilized for the focused task.

What "task orientation" means, then, is not that there won't be overlap some time or that a defined job for each individual forbids a sense of willingness to cross over and help in other areas. What "task orientation" does mean is that there is intelligence and order to the flow of work and the individual is provided with a sense of being closely fitted to what he can do well.

But such is not often the case at *Simon's Signposts to Glory Incorporated*.

3. *Status — Money*

If the worker at *Simon's Signposts* can't find status in position by his ranking within his department nor in the division of labor, he will look for it in his pay.

But he soon discovers that money is an even more complex area than any of the others. He begins to sense that double image about money emerging day by day. At morning devotions money is prayed against in terms of "the love of it being the root of all evil." But at the ten o'clock sales meeting, it suddenly becomes the "lifeblood of our survival."

He will thank and praise God with the president "over the fact that God has allowed us to make substantial profit again this year, which means we have met His standards for the proper ordering of our business affairs." But if he should get up the courage to ask for a measure of that to bring his salary up to some level on par with the inflationary spiral, he will be informed "that God blesses us only as we are willing to sacrifice as ministers entrusted with the dispensing of the Good News."

Money, then, is "evil" on the spiritual level, but "it is our life" in the physical sense. Money is a "trap," and yet "a necessary tool for carrying on the work of God." Money isn't everything, and yet "without it the company is nothing." The plain "dollars and sense of it" to the rank and file is that even Christian work follows in that order.

For Simon, "money is God's way of showing us we are on course, that our sails are properly trimmed, our conduct above reproach, our product that which He has confirmed as being His." In a sense, he's right; often God does bless in this way.

But what it says to the worker comes off differently. If the worker is so short-changed in his pay envelope week by week, a pay scale that is often so far below that of the same job in secular work — a pay scale that often allows him to remain only one step above the poverty line, then it seems that God has simply not chosen to smile on him in the same way He has the company.

Most workers know that it is one thing to work in a situation that is pinched in its profit return, and in that case they accept the stringency. But when a company is coming through to a profit of hundreds of thousands of dollars a year, it is naturally difficult not to see some of that "blessing" in his own pay envelope.

There is supposed to be some kind of "fringe benefit" at Simon's, but nobody knows for sure what that is. "The only fringe benefit I've seen is what I get at the coffee break," one employee says.

There is a company insurance plan, but it is mainly for "burial." There is that "hospital plan" that is "a $250 deductible which means just about every part of you has to be deducted before they pay." But at least it's all "economical."

There is no pension plan, because that is "installment buying on old-age mansions and smacks of unbelief in

119

the imminent return of Christ." If Christ should choose not to come in that generation, the worker will retire with some fanfare in the coffee room, a decorated cake, and a new Bible with his name engraved on the cover. Added to that is the final benediction: "You have fought the fight, you have kept the faith; now there is laid up for you a crown of righteousness which no man can take away." The worker appreciates it, of course. But his fight is not over by any means. With only a flimsy social security check to fall back on now, he will be forced into a cramped camp trailer on a crowded lot to live it out "for the duration," his battle with mere survival a gigantic one.

On the other hand, those who work in the "nonprofit" organization have a much better percentage going for them, for the church will at least feel somewhat "beholden" to them and see to it that some kind of retirement home or center is in the offing.

But strangely, at Simon's, for the man affiliated with the "profit making" business, his fortunes must ride on the provision of the president himself. And at sixty-five, "it done run out."

In the meantime, the short pay envelopes are rationalized on the principle that employees are expected to trust God to provide. But nobody knows what that means. Does it mean that if a man has sensitive or compassionate relatives, he may live on handouts from that direction? Does it mean that if he has a wife strong enough to work, he'll make it for sure then? The children will get farmed out to day nurseries and babysitters and grow up sucking their thumbs to the age of thirty, but "at least God was faithful in supplying our needs." Or does it mean working the night hours on another job? He wouldn't see his family as often, but "at least they'd make ends meet." On the other hand, there is a rule against "moonlighting" at Simon's, because that "smacks of a failure to trust God to honor His own, and what's more, a man won't be much good to me in this vineyard if he's been up all night working for someone else."

A man could get up the courage and ask for a raise. Not "big money" at all — just enough to meet his needs. But on that point Simon is quite dogmatic: "No raise in this company on needs — it is purely on performance."

But since there is no real sense of task orientation and no real measuring of performance in the company, how is the worker to judge his own contribution in those terms?

What it comes down to is that pay raises will come on the basis of longevity, how many years of "faithfulness and loyalty" to *Simon's Signposts to Glory Incorporated*. This does little to develop incentives or "mobility" in the work force, to say nothing of status. "He that endureth to the end shall be saved" is a Scripture that takes on a new meaning for the work force in those conditions, and it does not contribute to a good frame of mind.

The worker will forego the matter of "status" when it comes to position in the company or even in terms of "task orientation." His tolerance level is very high in these matters. But when a man takes his pay envelope home on Friday night to his wife and family, it's at that point that his "status" as a man faces a critical test. When he realizes that his wife and other "workable units" are throwing themselves into the line to make up the deficits needed to negotiate the simple matters of staying alive, he begins to experience that nagging doubt about his own "calling." It is at that point that he begins to realize he is not going to be ready when the emergencies arrive: sickness, birth, education, and the need to make certain his own growing children do not have to rationalize their own "lacks" on the basis of a "spiritually sacrificial father." A man like Billy Rawlson, for instance, does not really want "status" money in terms of two cars, a new home, or all of that which goes to the material levels. But Billy does want his five children to know that he, and he alone, as God's appointed head of the household, is fulfilling that role in the full dimension of provision. That's it.

There is a time and a place where a man must learn to trust God to make up the deficits. Most Christians know when. At the same time, there is also responsibility placed on the steward of that provision, Alexander Simon, to properly discharge his custodianship toward those who work God's vineyard.

It may be said that some of the larger Christian corporations, who sense the pressure of needing to attract better skills for the organization, have learned to come to terms with at least that much. Though it is not entirely satisfactory, at least it is an attempt to right the balances.

But for the "in between" groups, moving from smaller to larger, the remunerations continue to remain in that "frozen state." No one can properly explain why this attitude toward wages continues. If any organizational entity should be "ideal" in any factor or facet of its employer-employee relationships, it certainly should be the Christian enterprise. Why there couldn't be a model program of "profit sharing" in its fullest sense, at least up to a certain percentage, in a reasonably profitable Christian business is baffling. Why the "Christmas ham bonus principle" could not be translated into a meaningful profit percentage once a year defies explanation. The nature of the organization, as Christian, begs the gesture.

The peculiar stance he takes regarding money comes down to Simon's own double image about it. It is the most difficult aspect for him to properly relate and reconcile in his own mind, and again points up the complications of the shift from the ministry to the business-ministry. Having been raised in the "ministerial" sense of money, where it came down as manna from heaven (which was strictly donor sources in terms of the church offering plate), his handling of it was on the comparatively simple dimensions of "in and out." But now money has taken on a new image. What he has is not "donations" but "profit." Profits mean new complications in the uses of money — there are more demanding areas that legally require their part of it. There must be strategy to use it for increased productivity, which in turn guarantees more of the same. In the profit context, money has to be looked upon not simply as a "necessary evil," as in the days of the pastorate or even the garage, but must be viewed as a "negotiable instrument" for buying and selling without which he could not survive.

But Simon does not cross over to that arena of profit values. "The Lord giveth; the Lord taketh away" is still his mind set. This can only breed a total lack of responsibility for that which has been entrusted to him by God.

In a sense, Simon refuses to look upon his profits as profits. Perhaps he feels guilty that he is making money on a spiritual product. To compensate for that, then, he will continue to operate an austerity program, to make certain no one on the outside gets the impression that Simon's is a rich company. He will make certain there are no lavish displays of wealth or ostentation. And he will keep his own employees on the short string to buttress that point — for by maintaining his own work force on lower wage scales, he can perpetuate the image of sacrifice, deny that money really means anything, and thereby keep the spiritual balance in all things. Whether this assuages his sense of guilt about making profits, nobody knows.

Or Simon may rationalize short wages on the basis that "the less we pay out in operating costs, including wages, the more we have to plow into the product." The logic does not hold true. For if the worker is denied compensation even in terms of need, the constant pressure of "not making ends meet" is bound, ultimately, to cut into production effectiveness. What happens is that more and more workers quit and new ones have to come in to learn those jobs, which puts that aura of jerkiness into the work flow. The fact that Simon operates 50 percent under capacity is no surprise then, but it is a point he chooses to ignore.

But though these may be suggested explanations, nobody really knows what accounts for the peculiar bind with regard to employee wages that continues to have a stranglehold on the Christian organizational "sense of well-being." Workers are confused and demoralized by it. To complain about money constitutes a "mercenary spirit," and they know it. To ask for a raise seems to connote "inferior motivations in the Lord's work" and leaves them feeling guilty.

At the same time, the Christian worker has the spirit to adjust to stringency of wages if his superior explains the justifiable reasons for it. Every worker is fully prepared to "sacrifice" where he has to; he knows that Christian work does not offer him the heights of material prosperity. He does not seek that at all, but works within the organization for other values. But the president who exploits these "other values" as an excuse not to pay on the basis of performance or whatever criteria he uses is betraying the trust God has placed in him as a steward of money *and* people.

The successful Christian organizations have learned to articulate and define those "justifiable reasons" to the total rank and file. One organization shares the yearly profit and loss statement and takes the time to outline projected budgets, showing expenses as against income and how much is left to spread across wage increments. This attempt to be honest has accounted for a spirit of genuine "togetherness" in keeping with the proper vineyard principle. Simon's attitude — he believes sharing in this fashion "only gives people the wrong impression about the state of money in this company and will lead to more complaints about getting their share" — is an indication of his own failure to understand what is the heart of Christian work. It but supports his innate inability to come to a position of trust toward those who have entrusted their own lives and futures to him.

Finally, then, having failed to arrive at "status" in any of the three critical test points, why do so many stay? True, many have left, but it is interesting to note that the turnover in employee personnel has not hit the total work force with equal devastation. It is noticed less within the executive positions and those in some proximity to that area.

The fact that key people remain at Simon's has to do with their tenaciousness for no other reason than for the product. These people realize and work with the sense of loss in their jobs, salaries, and positions, the failure to sense any mobility within the departmental achievement profile, and the plaguing aura of disorientation in goals and values only because they sense that God has to be somewhere in it all. This is their primary "sense of call." If God is not in it, surely He must be in the wings, taking note, and will right the balances. Meanwhile, they learn to keep their eyes up and beyond Simon — or at least they try — and his idiosyncrasies in organizational management and draw upon those inner resources that God has given to them. There are still thirty thousand bumper stickers a day to get out, all of which they believe in the end will have some impact on the masses. To them, there is still tremendous "potential" in what they are doing, even in what *Simon's Signposts to Glory* can do to fulfill its destiny under God.

So they will laugh and cry and argue and complain — but in the end they stay. Not because they couldn't find anything better, with better pay and better "status" in the terms here discussed; they stay because of that "still, small voice" that says "if not you, who?" They stay because they entertain the optimism that what God shapes, He can reshape, including Alexander Simon.

They stay because to quit is some kind of admission that God isn't big enough to alter the "state of the disunion." They stay because of their conviction that they have come into the "kingdom for such a time as this" and such a place. It is not their choice perhaps, but in realizing that God had something to do with it, they will do their best to fulfill whatever He had in mind.

This is no endorsement of Simon necessarily, who thinks this kind of "loyalty" is a vote of confidence in his leadership. This is no "mandate" for him in his de-emphasis on the human elements upon which God puts His highest value.

It is, on the contrary, evidence again of the high tolerance of pain which the Christian worker possesses in the frustration he faces daily in unrealized values.

It indicates the mystery of the Kingdom of God in terms of the tenacity of its human elements to find some link-up with each other in fulfilling the Great Commission, as nebulous as it appears to be at times, and thereby to sense something of Cause.

It proves again the fantastic sense of endurance the children of God own with respect to the pressurizing forces that hinder them in their drive to put order as well as spiritual bumper stickers into the cosmos.

It illustrates again their determination to face up to the "cost" which is peculiar to their "missionary cause," a "cost" which is not an absolute set by God at all (it would be much easier to bear if this were true), but a "brain drain" and an "emotional squeeze" that come as the peculiar by-products of leadership not fully aware of the nature of the vineyard principle.

Finally, it is a classic example of their intense desire to find within the anthropomorphic dimension of the Christian organization a new sense of purpose, and beyond that a new sense of love and even freedom. Though what they may be receiving is fractured at best, they press on knowing that they see "in a glass darkly" but that it must become clearer — if God is anywhere near — and that clarifying that image is as much their responsibility as it is Simon's.

And strangely enough, they stay because of Simon. For while they recognize the human failings of the leader and are often victimized by him, they still sense that in him, ultimately, God has chosen to put His own reputation on the line. They sense, more than Simon does, the inner potentials of their leader, the possibilities of greatness, the resident energies that once harnessed by God could change the entire landscape of their everyday service.

They stay because there are those moments, too, when beyond the hectic, confused, disoriented beat of the uphill freight train called *Simon's Signposts to Glory Incorporated* there is that "sense of fulfillment, of victory, of accomplishment." Rare as these feelings may be, the fact that they do come, as blessed as "raindrops on the head," is indication enough that God has not yet abandoned the ark into the ditch.

Simon can take no credit for this, but it is within his province to build on that tenacity of spirit if he has the sensitivity to become aware of it. Until he does, he will remain the poorer.

But meanwhile, the "status complex" has to be lived with until that time when Alexander Simon arrives at his moment of truth. No one knows how long the human frame can bend and not break, even in Christian work. The evidences of fatigue in mind, spirit, or emotion are not always easily visible. The Christian worker can manage to hold together when his fight is clearly outlined as being against "spiritual darkness" and that which is purely "satanic." He begins to crack, however, when he realizes that the source of his struggle often emanates from the "human God center."

Meanwhile, he will go on to reconcile this in his mind as "human frailty," subject to change, and continue to travel "up the down staircase" in his uncertain journey to whatever it is he is pursuing, which to him can be found nowhere else except in the Christian organization.

And God chooses to continue to brood over the uncertain course of *Simon's Signposts to Glory Incorporated.*

VI

The Law and Order Complex – We Like Sheep?

For any organization to finally survive at all, it must have a sense of order. Order comes from establishing a line of authority figures (not authoritarian) in whom is placed the *recognized* responsibility for overseeing work performance and providing a force for continuity and cohesion. Once a company allows itself weakness in authority lines — or is not careful to structure them — it invites anarchy.

One of the problems in Christian organizational relationships is that each worker comes into the group with his own sense of "God-given authority." He feels equal to everyone else in his spiritual "call" as well as his spiritual relationship to God. In this sense he comes in with a built-in penchant to rule whether he is assigned authority or not. The adage "too many chiefs and not enough Indians" is more often manifested in the Christian organization than in the secular. To prevent that, the company director must set up the recognized authority lines immediately and constantly demonstrate his *trust* in them.

At *Simon's Signposts,* however, authority has never been fully given, and what is there does not have the necessary element of trust to support or reinforce it.

Actually, before authority is ever given, it must first be demonstrated. If Simon could not give authority to anyone, it was because he had not learned how to use it himself. In the first place, his concept of authority was shallow, based purely on the "law and order" manifesto and applied mainly in the area of overseership of performance and conduct. But for law and order to prevail, the authority figure must rule on much more important areas if he is to get the trust of those under him:

1. The authority figure, in order to hold his work force together under his leadership, must earn his right to authority by *building attitudes of trust* toward those under him. It is a two-way street — the people will learn to trust him, if he first demonstrates trust in them. (Later on this one factor is a critical test point in the "law and order complex.")

To get that trust, the executive takes into full account the total needs of his work force. This does not simply mean in the area of adequate equipment, supplies, and a proper sense of task orientation. It also means being accessible to all of the employees in their grievances and complaints and a readiness to settle personality clashes — and he must do this without breaking confidences.

2. The authority figure builds trust from his work force when he carries the responsibility for their failures, not just their successes. This means he must share the successes with them, which is the easy part, but at the same time take the blame himself for whatever goes wrong. The executive who passes the buck to the weaker links in his department is short-circuiting their confidence in him.

Antony Jay in his *Corporation Man* put it this way: "The leader is responsible for what his group achieves.

A consequence of that is that the leader will never excuse the group's failure by blaming a member of his group to superiors. He accepts that the group's failure is his failure."

This does not mean that the individual who failed is ignored. The executive will see to it that his authority is articulated in taking firm steps to make certain that failure does not occur again.

The weak point in Simon's authority line, if there is such a line, is an inability to take blame and consequently not owning up to the failure for what it is. The tolerance level to failure is too high at Simon's, because the "spiritual responsibility" toward failure is not really defined. The "B-attitudes" simply do not apply to sloppiness, chronic lassitude, or just plain laziness. People don't want to be "spiritualized" when they know they've committed errors any more than a child wants praise when he knows he should be disciplined.

The frustration attendant to this comes out in a sign in Simon's warehouse which is intended to be a spiritual reminder to deal with such matters as shoddy work performance:

BEFORE YOU SAY IT, IS IT GOOD?

And underneath was scrawled the foreman's reply:

NO, BUT IT'S NECESSARY!

3. The authority figure, in order to win his authority credential, must learn to use the spiritual and the business solution in proper balance. He has to learn that his subordinates do not wish to be clubbed with spiritual oversimplifications any more than they want corporation law thrown at them regarding a primarily spiritual matter.

When the authority figure learns to know the difference between the problems and the applications, he begins to build group trust in his leadership.

4. The authority figure in the Christian organization must be careful to maintain his relationship with his

subordinates somewhere between necessary informality and the formal attitudes of command.

In the Christian organization there is greater tendency to expect a certain "intimacy" with superiors in keeping with the "we are all in Christ" relationship. But the leader who indulges this attitude too far will lose respect from his group. The group needs to know when to use the informalities in the relaxed atmosphere *as set by the leader* and when to maintain a proper deference to leadership command.

Christian organizations like Simon's are remiss in their relationship to authority, but only because the company's main line directorate has set the tone for that in the first place. When subordinates are arguing with the department heads, changing specifications, altering elements of the work flow as supposedly set by the chief, there is an organization in trouble. Somewhere the control has slipped, and it is usually due to a failure of the appointed leader to set proper guidelines with regard to the attitudes expected from his workers in terms of job and group relationships.

The Christian business enterprise, by the nature of its "familiarity" in the Body, has to work hard and with certain decisiveness to build this authority. It takes sensitivity, understanding, and a firm declaration to hold the line at all costs. Employees look for it, expect it, even demand it. If it is soft spirituality, easy-come-easy-go command, the entire core slides into mush.

Simon never declared it, spelled it out, or even delegated it. He did not do that because his own concept of authority was built solely around his "custodianship" of the company. It was, in fact, a one-way street.

With authority lines undefined, except that everyone knew "who was boss at the top," all the other contingent elements of the "law and order" principle stood on very shaky ground and a new set of "complexes" began developing:

1. *Communication*

The most important element, together with authority, for holding a company together in some kind of unity of purpose is the communication system. People need to know what is being said by whom with what expected results. When this is clear, then communication with each other is much more meaningful.

The difficulty at *Simon's Signposts,* however, is that the communication flow is constantly *downward,* from the "control tower" to executives to the common herd of sheep. This is in keeping with Simon's vertical structure of authority — the "Alpha and Omega" syndrome, where all things begin and end with the president.

This one-directional flow of communication also stems from Simon's concept of the vertical relationship with God, who does "all the talking," while the child of God simply "does all the listening." In the spiritual closet by himself, the Christian does not mind that at all. But in a complex interweave of human relationships hung together around the demands of pressuring production schedules, there has to be some way to make oneself heard to the man at the top, whether he be Simon or the department head. And for that matter, isn't God interested in that "two-way" communication with His own anyway?

Drucker points out that such communication "is practically impossible if it is based on the downward relationship. . . . The harder the superior tries to say something to his subordinate, the more likely is it that the subordinate will mishear. He will hear what he expects to hear rather than what is said."

Rather than that strictly "downward pitch" in communication, Simon needed to cultivate the horizontal diffusing pitch, bringing his department heads into collective decision making with him on the major issues that affected the company's well-being. This is all a part of the *trust* factor that is paramount to building effective communication. The vertical, one-line flow of communication is synonymous with mistrust because, in essence, it says no one else is competent to affect the company's course or to look after its cardinal interests. The "God figure" syndrome then manifests itself in total stultification.

When this one-line flow of communication is entrenched, there emerge bizarre "systems" or vehicles for carrying out that communication. At Simon's it was the "memo syndrome." The interdepartment memo became the primary vehicle for communication to rank and file. Rather than direct confrontation which would make the word much clearer and establish rapport, Simon found the memo almost like writing the "tables of the law" all over again. It was not unusual at any time of the day, then, to see department executives plowing through reams of memo paper that had either come down from Simon himself or from other department heads who had long since copied the system.

The "memo" is actually designed to be a mental jogger or reminder, not a critical communication about core matters that have to do with major decision making. Simon's "memos," however, were drum rolling and trumpet blaring, so it was not surprising to see the confusion attendant in the constant rush to fulfill them.

The "memo syndrome" explains how *Simon's Signposts* came to have so much toilet paper on hand, stacked in every conceivable nook and cranny of every closet. It came about as a result of one of those "memo communiques" which started with Simon's writing up a request for

15 bx. M.P.

In this case "M.P." meant memo paper. But by the time it passed through the five departments, hunting for that area where memo paper was supposed to be handled, it took on a kind of "communications osmosis." And it is a known fact that in organizational memo streams, communication does not "produce after its kind."

The memo finally landed in Billy Rawlson's broom closet, and probably rightly so, for it now read:

150 cs. T.P.

Billy Rawlson was not about to question the memo, since it showed the president's office as "point of origin." Thus *Simon's Signposts to Glory* took on 1,800 rolls of "strange cargo," enough to keep a battalion in the field for a year. Later on it would constitute a "sizeable disposable asset" for the accountants who would be looking for liquifying equipment and supplies to help cover the company's deficits. But in the meantime there was still no memo paper. And even if it finally got ordered, there would be no place to put it.

There is some "happy insanity" about the "memo syndrome," but it takes on dimensions of the macabre when it becomes the main system of communication in the interdepartmental jungle. Simon, of course, used it to avoid direct confrontations with people, because he never won an argument or got the last word, as his history showed. But when department heads began to copy that principle, using it to avoid their own confrontations with people where the subject might promise some tension, there was bound to be a breakdown of some serious import. It was not unusual then to see departments carrying out their private "wars" with other departments only a few feet away, "stating their case" in crisp, full cap block letters of an IBM typewriter. The "paper war at *Simon's Signposts*" was soon coined, and it did not lift anyone's morale.

The "memo syndrome," of course, is bound to affect the total communication problem between people. Other organizations may revert to "courier service," where the secretary to the president runs commands and counter commands down the line of departments. Some use the "hot line" approach, a special buzzer that gives off a peculiarly raucous sound when it's the president on the other end.

All of these point to a major flaw on the part of the top man who seeks to control by devious means, forever forcing an atmosphere of shadowy omniscience when in reality it is an inability to cope with a proper interpersonal exchange.

The rank and file, caught in this kind of syndrome, lose confidence in themselves and each other's ability to relate. A sense of mistrust results and runs through the warp and woof of organizational relationships. If *Simon's Signposts* never reaches the ideal of "togetherness," it can be traced in a large part to the imbalanced, confusing, and often crippling level of communications.

Christians, especially when working in situations that have no status in terms of position, job, or pay, need the solace that more meaningful communications can instill. That kind of communication must come from the top. It cannot be the "missile firing" kind of thing Simon has adopted from behind closed doors. It cannot be constructed out of the "monitor type" of stance either — which is often Simon's rule with regard to his people; in other words, the president "monitors" work performance from his "plot room," and as long as everything is going well, no one will hear from him. But when anything goes badly, the "hot line" or the "memo" is immediately felt.

If Simon is to arrive at constructing meaningful communications, he must first become *visible* to his people. The head of a large secular manufacturing concern makes it a point to go down among his work force at least once a week, asking personal questions about them, their families, and anything about their jobs they don't understand or if the equipment is satisfactory. This develops rapport and a certain unmistakable esprit among the workers and begins to build a two-way communication system that allows for exchange with top management.

Simon must begin, however, by establishing his lines of authority, building trust toward his employees and they toward him. He can begin to develop trust in the work force by opening the channels of communication.

At any rate, the "law and order" principle that somehow was supposed to come out of this "memo syndrome" or "monitor syndrome" is pretty well shattered.

2. *The Regimented Devotional*

If communication is to be established with the intent of building trust, and the "memo and monitor" systems constitute major failure at the very outset, the regimented devotional becomes another critical area of misplaced emphasis. It is particularly evident that the devotional life in a Christian organization is either to be the "building element" or else it is to be intrinsically destructive.

The people who come to work at *Simon's Signposts* have come fully expecting some level of spiritual guidance and inspiration. They are not interested in simply functioning in jobs, but they anticipate in the uniqueness of the Christian organization that element of spiritual value that will put meaning into the performances. To them this is expected to be a kind of "bonus feature" in terms of their own spiritual growth.

Simon, however, looks upon the eight o'clock devotion through his already fractured sense of "central control" for the sake of "law and order." Therefore, his "required devotions" are couched in that same attitude of mistrust. They become his means of "putting everybody straight about what God expects in this organization."

But more innate to the whole concept, and what builds resistance to the "regimented" aspect of it, is the inner conflict about "compulsory worship of God." The Christian senses that his own personal, individual relationship with God is the only arena he has left where he can exercise his freedom. There is the sound of brass, then, in any attempt to "force worship patterns." And whatever value is supposed to come from it is lost finally in this inner conflict with regard to its purpose and place.

Further, growing out of this is the impression that is communicated to the rank and file by this regimented worship — that is, that they are not mature enough to draw on spiritual resources on their own to affect their day by day posture as Christians. The fact that they all have had their own prayer times at home regarding the day's activities does not seem to suffice. Only the company itself can "legitimatize" the spiritual devotions of its people. This reduces the sense of individual responsibility and brings out the "sheep syndrome" to its lowest dimension.

Beyond that, of course, is the apparent communications intent of Simon in the way he uses the meeting — which is usually three times a week when he's in — which is, whether by intent or default, geared to strengthen the president's hand in maintaining control and centralizing the fundamental spiritual predominance of the business.

In this "protective custodianship" intent, then, the devotional under Simon becomes more of an attempt to silence or neutralize complaints, grievances, and constructive criticisms rather than create an atmosphere of worship. The "devotional" too often becomes a kind of applying of the spiritual asbestos to the rank and file, forcing the employee to "think spiritual." What happens is that the employee begins to second guess himself in terms of any intent of bringing into the day's work some considered physical answers to physical problems. What may be legitimate grievances about job conditions and production, totally apart from the matters of pay, etc., are shuttled aside as "too mundane." He builds within himself that certain "bottled up" feeling which stems from his guilt in thinking any other way than spiritual and his frustration in not finding a safety valve for all of it.

But what makes the regimented devotional even more bizarre at Simon's is that every employee "must get a crack at devotionalizing." This often means that those who are not winning in the "paper war" within the daily interdepartmental struggle will now thunder their vengeance, beat their chests, and roar their spiritual tirades in various modes of eloquence, all in the name of the Lord. They may find some sense of therapy in this, while those who sit stoically in their chairs take on a certain glaze in their eyes which means shock is setting in.

The idea that "everyone must take his turn" can also create unnecessary pressures and sometimes even demean. Two days after Morton Hargrave was given his "sideways promotion" from Comptroller to Supervisor of Maintenance, it was "his turn" to take those morning devotions. It took some courage to be so exposed before the entire rank and file, who already knew of his unfortunate slide, and then to try to give spiritual meaning to it from the text: "Promotion cometh neither from the east, nor from the west, nor from the south. But God is the judge: he putteth down one, and setteth up another" (Psalm 75:6).

Or, as is often the case, there is the shipping room clerk who is not skilled in any sense to dig anything meaningful from the Word for public consumption. Having gotten up to face the rank and file, many of whom were in their forties and fifties, he simply said, "Today is my thirtieth birthday." He paused, looking at them intently, then added, "So what's left of life?" Thus ended his epistle for the day, and he promptly sat down. When someone, unable to contain himself any longer, let out a strangled kind of laugh, that saved the day for the clerk, though everybody else felt as if they were indeed on borrowed time.

The required devotions run from a point of manipulation for the president to a kind of platform for individual soul rending. They move on an uneven ride from a constraining for "law and order" to a rather bizarre, even demeaning stance to one of peculiar humor. The mix is not a good one. What is communicated finally is a rather distorted image of God, emerging through a strained attempt to keep everybody on a proper spiritual course.

The more serious effect, of course, is that the employee, knowing that he has to be at those company devotionals anyway, will make that a substitute for his own individual relationship with God. If it were a good substitute, it still would not be a healthy practice. But the fact that it usually turns out to be totally inadequate will result in spiritual poverty. Beyond that, of course, is that the constant daily routine of it brings a crippling sense of familiarity so that the individual finds proper worship centers in his church life peculiarly humdrum.

The answer to this is not necessarily the scrapping of the "devotional guidance." But it will require a shift in emphasis on Simon's part. He could begin by taking off that "compulsory" element. By providing a "voluntary worship" at that hour, he would be taking off the intrinsic strain already attendant to it. He would run the risk, of course, of no one showing up for the "voluntary time." And if that did happen, then he would know for sure that what had been going on was a "bore" or else totally irrelevant to employee needs. From that point, he would know that he would have to work on the purpose of such meetings and design them for the full inspiration of his staff, and no more.

However, the best thing he could do would be to knock out the daily required devotional altogether, as some successful Christian organizations in the ministry-business have done. In doing so, these organizations have first taken a positive position of trust toward the employees, believing that those who work in the company have the intelligence and spiritual sensitivity to keep themselves alive and right with God. What they do, then, is set aside one day a week, usually Friday, for a "company convocation." It is not set for eight o'clock in the morning so that it appears to be a "tack on meeting" or designed for a "spiritual overlay"; rather, it is set at ten o'clock, thirty minutes blocked out for the entire staff to share in. By taking company time, then, the meeting fits into the continuity of the company business. It becomes a kind of "refreshing break" for the employee, because the company administration is actually willing to cut thirty minutes for the benefit of all.

In this Friday "convocation" the program is designed to be a progress report on company development and problems. Second, it is a time of *sharing* in a spirit of honesty before God of personal problems or joys experienced in the course of the work day. The company is willing to "run the risk" on this openness — the risk, of course, being that it might become purely a grievance centered meeting — because the Christian organization is supposed to infuse and perpetrate this sense of honesty. But the "risk" doesn't compare to the feeling of participation and involvement the employee experiences by being allowed this sharing in the company "fortunes." The last part of the thirty minutes is given over to a brief word from the Scriptures, usually inspirational, and closes with a time of voluntary prayer.

The "convocation" idea is positively contributional by the company to the employee. It builds trust and respect. It is balanced between the problems of the business function and the spiritual motivation aspect. By sharing in it, the employee senses that he is an invaluable part of the total operation.

On the other days of the week, each department head is free to keep the first fifteen minutes of the day open for the "devotional" needs of his own people. This again is voluntary. Very few miss it, interestingly enough. They come because in that session they can learn to identify with the "humanity" and the "spiritual leadership" of the department supervisor in a spirit of informality. There is no "spiritual agenda," no immediate reading of a text, no "preachments." Again, the department head cultivates honesty and sensitivity within the context of the love of God, building a new sense of awareness to each other in the problems, anxieties, fears, or even blessings that are shared. At the end, he will simply read from the Scriptures and lead them in prayer.

The "devotional life" at Simon's could move to a point of successful communication if the design was changed in this way. At least the interpersonal communication lines would be established among the work force. In this atmosphere, there would be no need to carry on the "paper war." The openness of department heads to honesty, as demonstrated by Simon himself, becomes the key factor in this. Rather than trying to be a "spiritual referee" in the constant disputes and tensions, the department head now becomes a point of relief for the problems.

But, again, to allow for this kind of "open-ended" spiritual relationship, Simon will have to cultivate genuine *trust* first toward his executives and then to the total work force. He will have to trust their sense of spiritual maturity, their desire to grow spiritually within the company, and their longing to keep the spiritual balance alive in their everyday performance.

If he cannot trust them in this way, then he must fall back on authority, his own, to control it. Then he is in effect saying that his people are sheep in the total relationship to *him*. In that sense, he is actually robbing them of the "spiritual values" they need to learn for themselves. And in that, he may well be robbing God of the joys He should be experiencing in seeing His own seek Him in a voluntary pursuit of godliness.

A Christian worker can afford to lose everything else, but he becomes testy when he feels his spiritual values slipping. Few are willing to abandon that for the sake of "law and order."

3. *The Pledge*

If the communication of "law and order" does not come off in the regimented devotions, it is at least written clearly enough in the "company statement of spiritual conduct." The "pledge," or "hedge" as it is called at Simon's, is still considered to be the most sacrosanct line of prose in the entire framework of creative genius within the company. It is the constitution-and-by-laws, the rules of the road, the charter for the "promised land" of a separated life.

The pledge reads: "In keeping with the purity of *Simon's Signposts to Glory Incorporated,* as an employee, I hereby covenant to abstain from such worldly practices as card playing, indulgences in alcohol, films, theater, and any modes of dress or demeanor that would compromise the name of God and bring disrepute to this His vineyard."

To be employed by Simon's, of course, one must sign the "covenant" to "insure that no element of corruption will in any wise cause us embarrassment or put the name of God into question." It then becomes the code to maintain the "spiritual rightness" of the company. Everything else will come second to that in priority. There may be times in company "business" practices when ethics are played with, corners cut, bills unpaid, workers underpaid, and exaggerated claims made about the "power of Simon's Bumper Stickers to sock 'em in the eye with the Gospel," but these, apparently, have nothing to do with the "purity" of the organization.

Actually the pledge is to serve as the same controlling spiritual factor as the regimented devotions. It says that where the regimented devotion is to "insure the proper spiritual attitude inside the company," the pledge is to "make certain of the right spiritual conduct outside." Both underscore Simon's lack of trust in his people.

The pledge "hurts" even more than the other, however, because it forces the working credo into the living credo; it makes the company a perpetual encroacher on the total man, invading his personal and family life with inflexible proscription. It says, "Your home is not your castle, it is mine, Alexander Simon's." The pledge says,

Even then the employees don't argue with the existence of this kind of "covenant." After all, they signed it. What they mind is the words that are cast into inflexible dogma, allowing no room for change as the culture forces changes in the "taboos" on the part of the church. What they mind is that any organization, as such, should be allowed to legislate matters of conscience in conduct, as if they were a "company of sheep" who would plunge over the cliff rather than retreat.

An example of the problem of tension comes in the case of films. In any given week, Simon's has at least five film showings by outside companies seeking to sell Simon's buyers on their particular product. In those film showings the products are shown on "worldly backgrounds" such as ladies in bikinis or other such "fashions." These secular films don't hedge on scenes that show smoking, drinking, and even card playing at times, although they are in the "context" of illustrating the "power of plastics."

But though these exposures are allowed for the sake of the "company's product orientation," these same people are not permitted to view films outside for "personal enlightenment and creative stimulus." While they are not told to be "selective" in the film showings on the "power of plastics" inside the company, the pledge does not allow for any "selectivity" on the outside.

The "thinkers" find it more and more difficult to reconcile the double standard. It is not that they desire to rush off to every theater to view every "obscene or pornographic charade," but they want to be free from a restriction that really doesn't make sense. A false sense of "value" is beginning to add another layer on the already tight atmosphere.

The pressure on such employees becomes intense. They feel no condemnation in viewing the *Ten Commandments* on TV, but cannot "break their vows to the pledge" in viewing it in a theater. What one employee did was drive 150 miles to Poughkeepsie, New York, in order to see *King of Kings,* a film on the life of Christ. Does that presume then that he actually believed that God did not live in Poughkeepsie but only in Waldon?

No. As he put it, "I'll take my chances with God in Poughkeepsie, but not with Alexander Simon in Waldon."

Another "happy insanity" case was that of an employee who decided to break his pledge and see *Ben Hur* at a local Waldon theater. After devising a clever disguise, he got in and found a seat. When the lights went down, he removed his disguise, feeling he was quite safe in the darkness. But when the intermission lights came on again, he glanced around rather nervously and, to his horror, saw his departmental supervisor sitting three rows behind him.

In sheer panic, in fear of "being found out and having my job on the line," he roared down the middle aisle and blew through the side exit, almost breaking his leg in the process. While standing against the brick wall outside, nursing the bruise, it suddenly dawned on him that his supervisor was *still inside.* Since both of them were guilty in the same fashion, how could one charge the other without incriminating himself?

Thereupon, bruises and all, he stormed back into the theater and dropped into the same seat just as the colossal chariot race, the climactic point of *Ben Hur,* began. Five minutes later, he hazarded a glance behind him. His supervisor was gone! What confirmed in his mind that his boss had bolted the theater after seeing his subordinate three seats in front was the fact that his wife still remained, apparently unwilling to give up the chariot race for a point of debatable organizational code. But the fact that she was halfway under the seat trying to hide and yet still catch glimpses of the screen action was proof enough that she too was hurting from the horns of her dilemma.

What lengths doth man pursue for one solitary, innocent indulgence?

Actually the hopes of building stability and confidence in an organization by the irreconcilable rationales for "spiritual law and order" based on regimentation or proscription is almost totally frustrating. It breeds tension, guilt, and repression. It cuts into work force energy and sets up false value systems.

The successful Christian organizations — and there are those — who recognize the complexities of personalities in a ministry-business have cut the *specifics* of conduct pledges. Instead, their simple "pledge" is as follows:

> In all matters of faith and conduct, I hereby seek to govern my life as God would have it, doing all to the glory of Him. Wherein I cannot conscientiously imbibe in any practice or activity that does not fulfill that mandate or that which poses any question of that fulfillment, I shall seek to avoid it as potentially injurious to my Christian conscience and ultimately deleterious to my Christian growth.

This "statement of covenant" puts the responsibility on the employee himself, not on the company. It is a statement of trust that the employee will seek to conduct the matters of his own spiritual life *before God* and not before the organization. In so doing, it becomes "freedom in responsibility." This does not force Christianity into a non-biblical stance of "naming specific sins." What it does do is underline the biblical *principle* of Christian walk in holiness and righteousness. Thus the company is accomplishing two things: one, it does not force a practice of holiness or "purity" to a few listed sins, but lays the responsibility on the employee to maintain his awareness in the totality of his life as pleasing unto God. Second, it is a token of the company's assurance of the maturity of the people it hires. It allows the individual such "freedom" to test and weigh and finally judge by the Holy Spirit in him, and in this way the company plays its complete role in developing not simply a product, but a person.

Any Christian organization that cannot trust to that

extent may have to seriously question whether God does indeed indwell and keep His own.

It also teaches one other critical fact that is so necessary to the Christian business enterprise, if it is not so held in the voluntary agencies where proscriptions seem necessary to the whole sense of Cause, and that is that the sensitive demands of the business cannot afford the time-consuming arguments within or without over the conflicts spawned so often by codifications of conduct. It cannot afford unnecessary guilt problems brought on by morbid introspections that so often go hand in hand with the defined listings of taboos. It cannot afford to lose the best minds so desperately needed to develop the corporation simply because of a "conscientious objection" to signing anything so legally binding on individual freedom before God. It cannot afford to create in its staff a value system on the shaky foundation of what the company is not — either spiritually or corporationally — because minds impaled on negatives tend to become alienated from the realities of positive contribution.

Erich Fromm comes close to the issue at hand when he says, "If religious teachings contribute to the growth, strength, freedom, and happiness of their believers, we see the fruits of love. If they contribute to the constriction of human potentialities, to unhappiness and lack of productivity, they cannot be born of love, regardless of what the dogma seeks to convey."

Or maybe the Apostle Paul put it out even more directly, "For the kingdom of God is not meat and drink; but righteousness, and peace, and joy in the Holy Ghost" (Romans 14:17).

4. *Decision Making — "It has been decided...."*

If communication is not properly established, if regimentation is used to make up for the lack of it, then the domino effect takes over. Every critical element of the organizational structure begins to feel it. One place where it eats away with corroding destructiveness is in the decision making process.

A Christian organization leader who has not demonstrated his trust by creating proper authority leaders for communication in the total sense is not going to get "law and order" even if he hires a sheriff. Law and order is tied inevitably to decision making, but if it is to come in its most healthy dimension, it emerges out of the collective contributions of the executive staff.

Executives make decisions — or they are supposed to — not the subordinates. There is no such thing, however, as a "single executive decision maker," as Simon has projected himself. Because he insists on this, out of fear that he "might lose control of things," *Simon's Signposts* continues to experience fantastic bottlenecks in work flow. "Decisions" are "up for grabs" in that kind of structure. Such simple decisions as the color of the checks, how many paper clips, and how much floor wax, as well as the more complex matters of product image, advertising, sales campaigns, and budgets are all funneled back to the top for the "signature of the big man."

The executives — or *the executive* as Simon is — do not — or should not — make many decisions, according to any management law. They cannot possibly do so and remain sane. Drucker says, "The effective executive concentrates on the important matters. He tries to think through to what is strategic and generic rather than solve problems." It is not for him to handle the "nitty gritty" of work flow, but to delegate all of that to those who are on the lower levels of department responsibility. Simon has supposedly put all of that "lesser nitty gritty" into the hands of his executive staff. And yet it is not unusual to see a whole array of products on his desk, sent up to him by departments for his "touch, taste, smell, feel," before anybody orders anything.

In the meantime, Simon still maintains that his executive staff actually determine with him the matters that are "generic" to the company in terms of the company's production and future course. And yet the decisions that are "generic" are no different than those that are confined to the texture of paint that is supposed to go on the flagpole. He, and he alone, as the "God figure" must finally "bear the responsibility."

What this costs the company in money loss is one thing. But what it costs in terms of the time element is another. There is no way that Simon can possibly keep up with the backlog of decision making situations that, he says, "must have his okay." Executives under him must wait their turn to decide on matters that are even peripheral, because nobody knows what he can get away with on his own at any given time. The "time drain" in the wait has cost the company dearly and will eventually build the design for ruin if not corrected.

Beyond that, the failure to communicate decision making power on lower levels demeans an executive's abilities in this regard, cuts his initiative, and eats into any semblance of authority he has tried to develop "in spite of Simon."

But, in the meantime, Simon tries to go through the motions of using his executive staff in this regard by calling incessant meetings.

The "meetings," however, are something else again. They are designed mainly to get "consensus" for what he has already decided to do. "Gentlemen, it has been decided," is his favorite opening. Decided by whom? By seeking "consensus" he simply reinforces his own impeccable powers regarding what is "right for the company." All he wants from his mute executives is support, approval, or acclamation. The critical areas of company policy as to future design of bumper stickers, new products, additional personnel, or creating of new departments are not decisions that one man can trust to himself. Such matters are bound to affect every department, and without knowing what the effect might be, the wrong decision could play havoc.

To this end Drucker says, "Decisions of the kind the

executive has to make are not made well by acclamation. They are made only if based on the clash of conflicting views, the dialogue between different points of view, the choice between different judgments. The first rule in decision making is that one does not make a decision unless there is *disagreement*."

This is "strange doctrine" to Alexander Simon's life style credo. Since his communication system is already established as a one-way street with no room for exchange, always downward, to turn it around now and open it to "dialogue" would be to declare his own sense of fallibility. And if he does not get his executives to enter into the meeting meaningfully or constructively, it is because they know he has that frozen sense of judgment, his alone.

To Simon, then, "disagreement" is resistance to authority. It "smacks of hostility and personal ambition" and breeds "murmurings and complaint which resulted in Aaron getting knocked down in the Old Testament when he tried that with Moses."

What "disagreement" could do for Simon would be to bring the creative powers and imagination of his executives to bear on the question at hand. By controlling or even "organizing" that disagreement, as Drucker urges, he could get the full spectrum of possibilities from which he could make the kind of decision that would have greater possibility of being best for all concerned.

As it is, however, the meeting turns out to be a "think positively" session. That means that the executives must see and support what Simon "has already decided to do." If by any possible mischance, as Pearl Munson dared to do at the hour of truth, any one of them should throw in a question about the "feasibility" or perhaps "the practical considerations of money" or that the "budget can hardly tolerate it," this gets the simple rebuttal, "Where is your faith?"

At that point there comes the pontifical spray over it

all, "This is what God surely wants us to do . . . so let's pray about it." The prayer becomes in essence another means of "positive reinforcement" for the decision, putting down any further element of disagreement. It has, then, been "forever set in heaven."

The executive goes out of these meetings stuck with a decision that he had no part in, but which is going to affect him later. When the "affect" does actually come, and should it result in putting his department in a bad light, then there is the "moment of reckoning" to Simon who now asks, "You have fallen 28 percent below production. How do you account?"

And if the executive begins to trace it back to that "decision" of Simon's months back, then comes the rather abrupt question, "But weren't you at that meeting?"

Again, to allow for disagreements as a necessary part in the major decisions takes trust. To call meetings to affirm what has been decided is disorganization at its worst and communicates the fact that the subordinate executive has become the prisoner of the company. He is locked into a system that allows for no contribution toward the future of the company or even to its present viability.

Further, if an executive actually manages to "win a case" and is given reluctant permission to implement a decision of his own regarding his department, the long arm of Simon continues to interfere. For after putting together the project as "cleared at the top," the executive moves on to other matters. Or he may mistakenly go on the road or take a day of vacation. In that interim, Simon, not sure that what has been done is according to his own "intuitive powers," will lay his hands on the project and change the total specifications "to fit." The executive finds out much later, to his shock and dismay, that what he thought was "his decision" was not at all. He is left with a classic example of the "law" of the organization reaching out with a heavy absolute hand, but with no consequent sense of "order."

It is then understandable why over the desk of the "supervisor of production" at *Simon's Signposts,* who dares to run the risk of cynicism, there hangs a slogan which says, "The higher up the ladder you go, the more your tail is exposed."

The statement encompasses all structured situations that allow for any increment in responsibility in the work force. It also explains — even in the Christian organization — the growing resistance to take positions of responsibility without commensurate authority. It boils down to the innate need among executives for some sense of firm ground in what should be a position of trust.

There is, then, a fantastic freedom crisis that has emerged in the Christian organizations caught under the heavy hand of the Alexander Simons. The need for freedom is not freedom to disobey, encroach on authority lines, be indolent, shoddy, or, of all things, "unspiritual." Freedom is primarily seen by rank and file as a "need to emerge into self-awareness, to be creative, to share where I can share, to give where I can give, to be trusted where I can be trusted."

The failure of this priceless "freedom in the Body" to materialize is commented on again by Fromm when he says, "It is the tragedy of all great religions that they violate and pervert the very principles of freedom as soon as they become mass organizations governed by a religious bureaucracy. The religious organization and the men who represent it take over to some extent the place of family, tribe, and state. They keep man in bondage instead of leaving him free. It is no longer God who is worshiped but the group that claims to speak in His name. This has happened in all religions. Their founders guided man through the desert, away from the bondage of Egypt, while later on others have led him back toward a new Egypt, though they call it the promised land."

The increasing sense of "complex," whether it be

from the lack of status or the stricturing law and order overlay, can begin to erode seriously the Christian worker's personality and even his spiritual life. He will continue to try to laugh it off, find the "fun" in it all, and come to terms with it with what everybody is already beginning to sloganize, "After all, this is a Christian organization."

But the conflict in his life, building each day over the schizoid dimensions of the ministry and the business, can bring him to a near schizophrenic stance toward life outside as well. He senses that he functions as one type of human being in the office, caught in the dichotomy with its attendant pressures, and quite another at home and even in his church. He finds himself trying to communicate to his community the values and supremacy of the Christian way of doing things, but must face up to a nagging sense of doubt about it all in the office.

What this does is give him a pose of unhealthy defensiveness about his work, his worth, and his Christianity. The haphazard systems he is caught up with in his job give him very little sense of rightness, direction, or validity as to what he is as a "Christian worker." After a while, he begins to *accept* his doubts, worthlessness, and stumbling functionality as an absolute set by God. His mind begins to form a postulate from it all — that *maybe* it isn't supposed to be any different; that maybe *he's wrong* in his search for the values intrinsic to proper performance and worthwhile contribution; that perhaps his "ideals" are too far out of line with the *realities* of the Christian organization. Which means, as he pursues this too far, that maybe Christianity itself does not own up to whatever the ideals are, defined out of Scripture. He begins to mumble then: "Jesus, yes; the organization, no."

His "complex" becomes a point of serious conflict. From this comes the move to accommodate to "things as they are" and less of a desire to try to change what needs to be changed and could be changed easily enough. But in the resignation to the pressures, he also suffers a painful withdrawal into himself. In time, he senses alienation from the company in terms of primary concerns. He will function, move bodily through the daily routine, but it will be nothing but motion. To be reduced to that, when he had come to look for so many beautiful dimensions of achievement and fulfillment, is going to hurt deeply.

Erich Fromm summed it up succinctly when he said, "A few individuals can stand this isolation and say the truth in spite of the danger of losing touch. They are the true heroes of the human race but for whom we should still be living in caves. Yet for the vast majority of men who are not heroes, the development of reason depends on the emergence of a social order in which each individual is fully respected and not made a tool by the state or by any other group, a social order in which he need not be afraid to criticize and in which the pursuit of truth does not isolate man from his brothers, but makes him feel one with them."

It should be said, in all fairness to Simon and the Christian organization as such, that an employee can come to expect too much as well. There are those who will always look to the Christian organization as that "city of refuge" in which all the problems and pressures of life no longer hold credence. There are those who come with too much idealism, who lean too heavily on the fragile structure for life supports that should be drawn elsewhere. There are those who look to the organization as the *totality* of their life and purpose and function, and thus bring severe strain on the already weak straw of leadership. There are those, of course, who want to take everything from the organization and give nothing back.

The man or woman who looks to the Christian organization for service must come to know the difference between rightful expectation and quixotic idealism. If Simon is to change, he will do so only as there are such people who have learned this primary principle. In this sense, then, the employee has a responsibility as well. While he searches for and even pursues his rightful expectations, he is at the same time bound to bring balance and a sense of boundary to his own demands. The complexity of the vineyard and the frailty of the human leadership beg this level of compassion.

But the increasing weight of the problems does not rest in the lap of the employee. Usually, when the organizational management seeks to own up to its own responsibility toward the rank and file, they in turn will respond in positive fashion.

The big question remaining is: is there any hope?

VII

Will Success Spoil Alexander Simon?

In the light of all that has been revealed about *Simon's Signposts*, the question is whether the organization can ever really right itself enough to keep the "crew" from having to walk on a perpetual forty-five-degree list.

It may be said that it can't. That perhaps in the end, considering the awful cost accrued to attempt the voyage, it would be far better that the Christian culture not engage in the dual dimensions of ministry *and* business. Perhaps by the very nature of it being an ideology, and thereby not a "profit-oriented" community, it should seek to penetrate society with its "message" using the "nonprofit" organizational structure. At least in the latter sense the expectancies of the workers would not be quite so high, and in like manner perhaps Alexander Simon would not be forced into the fixed stance of spiritual authoritarianism.

The possibility is not without attractiveness. It has

been noted at the very outset of this book that there is a proliferation of "profit-centered" Christian manufacturing producing tons of products, much of which is of dubious value. The pull of the "money market" has led far too many Alexander Simons, totally unprepared, into the marketplace with the already evident and attendant debris strewn in their wake. In all of the fumblings and near capsize pitch of these groups, the image of God is what suffers the most, either in the people serving Him, as has been analyzed, or else in the product, or both.

Perhaps the "vineyard principle" in Matthew 20:1-16 supports the "nonprofit" consideration. For there the Lord controls the vineyard and pays as He wills, not necessarily on the hours put in, but on need, drawing on the resources He has available. This is the highly "unstructured" principle and does not carry with it the stresses of the "business."

On the other hand, there is Jesus' parable of the talents as recorded in Matthew 25:14-30. There the Lord gives so much investment to each man with the mandate to go out and "reproduce" or, in other words, "make a profit on that investment." The strains are far more evident in this "vineyard principle of business" than in the other, but the Lord sanctions both.

At any rate, regardless of which side of the argument one takes, will the shifting of *Simon's Signposts* from a "profit base" to "nonprofit" alter the basic problem of Alexander Simon? Granted that much of the failure in Simon's life is due to his inability to move from the "nonstructured vineyard-ministry principle" to the "business talent-centered structure," will the changing of that business principle alter the nature of the "complexes"? Perhaps somewhat. But even if the bumper stickers were to be produced out of a church-sponsored and church-financed enterprise, that still would not answer the basic problem of incompetency in leadership. There are just as many people suffering in the "nonprofit" vineyard under the peculiar caprices of "the Simon syndrome."

But more important in this consideration is the fact, noted earlier, that the Christian organization in its *business* profile has the potential of emerging as a "ten group," the significant key within the total "hunting band" of the church. The successful Christian-industrial groups have already proven that influence. It has been noted that the "ten group" is essential to the church, because such groups demonstrate the much needed model of collective energies united in the purpose of intersecting secular man with the "spiritual product." It has, in like manner, proven the point that the same energies can be harnessed for the edification of the Body, and people are willing to pay for it. The model is a catalyst to the church voluntary agency and a vindicator of the existence of such purely church-affiliated groups when so much of its activities seldom really penetrate effectively into the mainstream of the world.

The Christian business-ministry, then, has a role to play, a valuable one, and since it is probably here to stay, the answer is not to withdraw it from the marketplace or even attempt to clip its almost schizoid structure of ministry-business. What is needed, as has been attempted here, is an exposure of the problems in the hope that leadership will take time to pause and reflect, and in that reflection do some stocktaking.

The question is still there, however: Can *Simon's Signposts to Glory Incorporated* rise to that "ten group" stature in its obviously "palsied state"?

The answer is yes. There is, after all, hope.

The translating of hope to reality is, of course, Simon's in the final analysis. But it must be said, and importantly, that if God has laid His own reputation on the line with the Simons in Christian work, then He is not far "outside" any of them. For all of Simon's problems, for all of his authoritarian bent and life style credo, for all of his coddling of patriarchal fancies and theocratic controls, for all of his failures to evaluate, examine, and actually take stock of his resources, for all of his "rule of uncertainty," for all of the "complexes" he is going to instill, the amazing fact is that God will condescend to brood over him. That is one of the cardinal mysteries of the Kingdom of God, and yet it is the mainspring of hope.

Because beyond all of Simon's spiritual mind sets that are frozen in their mold is that vein that holds the "hidden gold" that can yet lift him and *Simon's Signposts* to greatness. Deep within the fat encasing the heart muscle is the clean line of that one solitary nerve that is ready to pulsate into life. Somewhere in Alexander Simon, and those like him, despite the record of missed connection in his past, the shaky emergence of his "revelation," the shallow level of his comprehension of the complexities of the vineyard he considered to be far too simple, there is yet something within that God is willing to use. It is that "something" that lies deep within, perhaps only one simple quality upon which God will attempt to build, provided Simon can work it out into the center of his top-heavy authoritarian stance. Perhaps it is tenacity, determination, dedication. Maybe it is, in essence, that same quality of "desire" that God honored enough to allow him his adventure in the first place. For Simon is not without that desire to be fair, liked, and respected. His actions that seem to breed the opposite of any of these attributes are not so blindly deliberate. He is a man being pulled and shoved by the forces set in motion in his life way back at the age of five. In a sense, he cannot help himself for what he is in that respect. But even in that, he is still held accountable for his refusal to evaluate all of it and know what has to be tossed aside. God will go with him on his desire, but not forever.

Yet God continues to wait for whatever it is that is lying there in the nondescript furniture of Simon's inner house. So do the rank and file. In a sense, they and God are "victimized" while they wait. God will prod and shape what is within His province to perform; but it is a rule of heavenly strategy that He will not redo what the man can redo, and must, for himself. God does not violate the capacities He has already put into His own in terms of self-judgment and the power to measure the length of his own line. God works according to the will of His own and seeks not to impose His will. The "will" to see himself, examine himself, and better himself must come from Simon himself if God is going to make any move toward him in altering the nature of his other poor powers. Simon will either use those innate faculties to affect his own course or else continue to build on bricks of straw. In the end, "Jesus will not commit himself unto him . . ." (John 2:23-25).

As for the rank and file, the enduring line of patience is conditioned on the degree of the "state of the complex." There is a point when a man or a woman has lost that "love of self" so critical to endurance. When the sense of individual worth slips away under the depersonalization rendered by "product orientation" (the message first) rather than "people orientation"; when the "vineyard principle" fails to provide some fix in the chaos of human elements outside; when order, logic, value, goals, purpose, and contribution are diluted, blurred, blotted out, and ignored, the "complex" becomes total loss. At that point, "Patience done run out." That man will flee for no other reason than to save himself, or maybe to save whatever he has left of God.

But in the meantime the rank and file seek to fulfill their responsibilities. At least most of them. A big part of their own lives is tied up in *Simon's Signposts* too. They know that Simon is because *they are*. They know what Simon apparently refuses to acknowledge, if he indeed really knows, that 30,000 bumper stickers a day are because *they are*. They know, too, what he won't or can't see — that he has the "potential" to take them all to what as yet has not been reached in terms of the "ideals" that are to be fulfilled in this God-given vineyard.

They know, in light of all that, then, that their charge is to "hang in there" and keep the smelling salts handy. They know that he is, in a sense, their "Joshua," although a "backfiring imitation patriarch at best."

They know Simon is clay as they are clay; he is human as they are human; he is a composite of the meager chemistry of flesh and blood and its attendant limitations, as they are. So in the knowing, as they are known, they believe that Simon must surely come to that point when humility possesses his glands and his stiff, ramrod, imperial carriage will begin to bend.

And they know, too, that there aren't enough Christians to go around — although Simon seems to believe there are — to continually replace those who fought "their good fight" and lost. Because in the end those who go out in defeat, having missed what was held out to them by God, are not advertising the "fringe benefits" at *Simon's Signposts to Glory Incorporated*. "There is none so fierce a man than he who has lost what he is rightful heir to," said Samuel Johnson.

But no one knows the length of any man's line in the "waiting" either. Simon continues to presume he will always have them, "complex or no complex." He still exploits their own sense of "call," still dares to believe that this vineyard is the best of all possible worlds to the Christian. His fixed concept of the worth of the individual against the priority of spiritual bumper stickers forbids him any other evaluation of them. Those who leave, to him, "never had dedication in the first place."

But the Christian working force is growing less patient with this presumption. The changes going on in the total social milieu around them, the reevaluation of themselves in their broader educational and technological pursuits will not keep them compliant to valueless administrative controls that are done in the name of God.

Marshall McLuhan said, "Technological changes recast the entire character of the individual and compel him to rediscover himself in depth instead of in detachment and objectivity."

In the future, the Christian worker, and it is already beginning to show up here and there, is going to insist on the right to rise to his own potentialities within the Christian organization. By the simple measurement of his own humanity and the consciousness of his God-given gifts, he will create the pressure for change. Blind obedience to archaic systems and controls that demean his sense of value as a person and as a servant of God are not to be tolerated forever. Christian work is not going to be seen as "just another job," but a place for enriching experiences. If these experiences are not present, they will institute changes to see that they are. They will no longer seek to use Christian work as simply a "legitimate means to find meaningful Christian service," but they will seek to experience within that group the fullness of the joys and beauties that God has put there for them. The Christian worker is going to pursue the intimate relationships with others that go with the Body of Christ wherever it is manifest in collective units. They will pursue that sense of community, above the jobs, and thus come to trust each other, love each other, and more assuredly look to each day with greater expectancy of fulfillment. Christian workers are already coming to that point in time when they no longer will quit an organization because leadership will not or cannot see the validity of these needs. They know that moving from one group to another is mostly empty pursuit, and there are not yet enough successful ones to absorb them. Instead, they will seek to shape the one they are in as best they can "within the system," making their expertise and knowledge too valuable to lose and thus wield more power to effect that reshaping. But to do that they will need a number of key, gifted, dedicated people within the group who own such expertise and value.

The possibility of change, then, lies in the caliber of people whom God must "call" into these organizations. That "call" is primarily for the gifted, trained, experienced, and spiritually mature executive, mainly from the secular business arena, who can successfully man the bilge pumps while trimming the sails at the same time. It calls for men and women who will go into these organizations with their eyes wide open, fully aware of the conditions, the complexes, and the heavy hand of the Patriarch. Such individuals will have to possess qualities of forbearance, patience, resolution, and sheer tenacity. It will take love, diplomacy, and wisdom of the first order to work with, through, or even around Alexander Simon — whichever it takes to get the Good Ship Grace on course. Mostly it calls for people who will not allow themselves in the process to be stripped of their gifts or their calling, but will make their talents and resources felt despite the heavy hand of the authoritarian. These specially anointed people must see their "calling" for what it is, not necessarily as a millennial experience or a Mount of Transfiguration, but a commission to put sweat, blood, and even tears into the often gritty mundaneness of business-ministry that is at best a confusing hybrid. And they must see Alexander Simon, not as their enemy or God's, who must be rudely bumped out of the organization to make way for change, but as a man, and still God's man oddly enough, who is a composite of tremendous needs, many of which he is not aware of himself. They must see him in his *potential*, then, as God sees him, and put their energies on the line to bring him to full greatness and the organization to rightful impact.

For such individuals the price may seem high. There will be defeat, despair, and the agony of total frustration. But is this so strange to any servant of God? And yet beyond all that there is the promise of ultimate change, the salvaging of lives, and the reward of eventually seeing "God's vineyard" fully operative in keeping with the image.

There is every evidence that such people — executive and rank and file — are already responding to God's constraint in this regard, and this emergence alone has sprung open the jammed doors of hope for the many inside who seek not simply deliverance, but direction.

In the meantime, of course, if the Alexander Simons can or will get into stride with the growing disposition of their workers now and the caliber of people whom God is sending to them for the future, they can be the architects for the total "redemptive process" rather than just being dragged along. It is not impossible. There is enough evidence to indicate that the Simons are beginning to sense the critical point in their own organizational health, even though it is difficult to admit. The sheer weight of competition has begun to rest heavily on the creaking timbers of *Simon's Signposts,* and this alone has begun to put cracks in the plaster. There is some indication here and there, feeble as it may be, that the Simons are beginning to sense that perhaps the best thing they have going for them are those "expendable" units who punch their timecards every morning. This is that other element of hope for the Christian-industrial organization.

But if the Simons will not rise to it, then these forces already at work will inevitably move the organizational course their way. In that case, as the future with its building pressures of competition and organizational strains demands dramatic moves for mere survival, the power will shift to the people with the expertise who will have to assume controls and leadership. Simon will remain the figurehead, the head of the body as it were, but only as he can complement the other working parts. For, again, as the worker develops a new awareness of his own skills and responsibility to the organization as one who has been *sent* by God, he is going to assert more pressure to make himself heard, to *contribute* realistically and meaningfully of himself and what God has given to him for the success of the group as a whole. If Simon is attuned to the steam already oozing out from that pressure cap and evaluates it properly and realistically, he could become the rightful leader to the yet unexplored vistas of creative and productive dynamic.

Meanwhile, of course, they "wait." While they wait, the light stays on in the sanctuary. Their waiting is the highest point of compassion that they can muster for Simon now, and only on that does the flickering flame of *Simon's Signposts* continue to burn.

The future, then, lies in how Simon views this "waiting." If he blindly accepts it as a tribute to his "leadership" without analyzing it for what it is, his "bumper stickers" will but articulate his own hypocrisy. For no man can glory in the fruit at the expense of the laborers who produced it. Those "sins" have a way of coming home to roost.

On the other hand, if Simon sees that "waiting" for what it is — enduring until he rises to the full stature as God intended — and then takes the first step to the alteration, he too can know fulfillment in terms of his people and the product.

The question is: Will success spoil Alexander Simon? Is the "success" of producing a few million bumper stickers a year finally going to "spoil" him? Can he stand much more of that "success" if it is interpreted as "God's blessing on the business"? Or is the "success" as the true measurement indicated here — in terms of the people producing it — going to diminish him in the end in terms of production? It is a question every Christian organization leader comes to sooner or later when he condescends to think about change.

It has been said here that Alexander Simon is a composite of the attributes that have plagued Christian leadership. It must be pointed out for clarification that the problem plaguing Simon, and those like him, was not that he was *too spiritual*. The problem was that he did not make "his calling and election sure" in terms of how to carry that spirituality over into the complexity of mundane business. He failed to measure the length of his own spiritual shadow against the demands of that arena and take to himself the resources needed to negotiate it. It was primarily his failure to see that the spiritual principle must be properly attuned to the nomenclature of the culture in which it is to operate. The business world "culture" changes in its methods and in the relationships of the people seeking to perform within it. The moral and ethical principles of spirituality can apply, but the hard line patriarchal, authoritarian leadership is going to leave skid marks all over the place, including the rank and file.

It was not that Simon's spirituality did not apply to the business, but that he did not wed the two in the kind of union where each could give separately to the other, complementing each other, and thus give balance to the total organizational course.

His problem was not that he had been a Christian from childhood, but that he did not make his journey to manhood in steps and stops where he could evaluate and reflect on the demands life would make of him as a spiritual being. (Even those who become Christians later in life have allowed themselves the "costly" leap from spiritual experience to the complexities and entanglements of the world without "counting the cost.")

His problem was not lack of intelligence even as he ruled according to the bent of his spiritually authoritarian mold cast upon him from his early years. It was fundamentally a case of "too many blind spots" in his world view, *which he allowed to remain,* and which shaped his total organizational ethos.

His problem was not that he was too quixotically committed to the product and the need to confront man with the messages. Rather, it was his failure, in that, to recognize the scriptural order of priority in all matters pertaining to the vineyard principle — people. Both of the parables in Matthew teach this imperative. Jesus started with twelve men, not twelve loaves of bread. He spent His time with those men, not in the "Gospel factory." Once those disciples came to full stature, clear in their minds as to their relationship to Christ, to each other, and to the Great Commission, and in that order, only then did the fire come down, and they moved into their "production roles" as such.

Simon had the order wrong. He is not alone in that, but that still offers no comfort. There are too many church agencies, profit and nonprofit, who take too much pride in the quantitative factors of *how many* candidates, workers, buildings, converts, or what have you, while at the same time ignoring the individual. Because so many of them share the same indictment does not justify them or their failures. What it does is heighten the state of calamity running through the entire Christian organization community.

So, then, the big question is this: Are there any *successes?* Yes! There are Christian-industrial organizations of various descriptions who have risen to their full stature as both a ministry and a business and have not compromised anything either way. There are others who have succeeded only when the leadership decided to make it a business and forget the constant attempt to put a spiritual overlay into it as a "ministry." Perhaps there is some credence to the latter concept; perhaps it is true that the *dual dimensions* of business-ministry can only lead to conflicts. It is certainly true, however, that the organizations who have tried to ignore the business end and stick to the ministry, as Simon did, have a mean tangle of problems.

But the fact that there are *business-ministry* organizations, or *ministry-business,* that have made it work is worthy of note. Interestingly enough, and significantly, those successful organizations have leaders who have passed through the "Alexander Simon syndrome." Many of them openly admit a point in their history when they found themselves in the authoritarian stage, the spiritual overlay stage, the spiritual control stage, and the "product versus people" stage.

What led them to finally "break out" from that paralyzing stance is also worthy of note. The over-all attributes for success are wrapped up in three necessary states of mind, or "changes of mind," with regard to their roles:

1. AWARENESS. It is not simply that the successful leader suddenly decides to do the opposite of what he has been doing as an authoritarian. The authoritarian seldom, if ever, does the opposite as long as the "God figure" mentality remains. If he is to rise above that, he must become *aware* of where he is and what he is doing, *not in terms of himself primarily,* but in terms of the totality of what is his care.

Awareness, to the strictly spiritual authoritarian leader, is that which is attuned *only* to the "spiritual sounds" within or without. All of his company, then, every function and person in it, passes through his spiritual screen. As important as that is at times, true awareness takes in all of the spiritual and physical dimensions. It sees not only saints, but workers. It sees not only the body, but the component parts. It hears not only "thus saith the Lord," but "please help me!" It senses not only the clatter of machinery, but the muted cry of "What does all this mean in the end?"

Awareness moves from the self-centered inside to the soul-centered outside. It is this that moved the Son of God from His Mount of Transfiguration to the valley of tears, hurt, confusion, and the desperate needs of people, and thus to a sense of *being needed.*

Awareness listens to the heartbeat of the collective body, and does not measure it according to his own, but makes theirs the measure of his. The sounds of leaky valves, pinching arteries, and the closing of the ventrical chambers stab him with the awful realization that he is responsible, for a leader in any corporation is the sum total of the health and well-being of its parts.

Awareness on the part of Simon could have saved Morton Hargrave the agony of years filled with the perplexing and confusing maze of never finding one moment of satisfying performance.

Awareness could have detected the bleeding inside Billy Rawlson, who only wanted to be a part of the "great adventure" of confronting man with the Word — but who at the same time felt a desperation to perform what he knew best — who struck out, having tried to express himself, to tell somebody that "he had a lot to give."

Awareness could have revealed the treasure in Pearl Munson — that in that quiet, steady spirit with so many administrative gifts was a significant key to carrying *Simon's Signposts* a long way toward the vineyard goal in terms of true value and purpose.

Some leaders don't or won't cultivate awareness. Some of them don't know how. In that case, the successful Christian leader, really concerned enough, can call in the outside "company analyst" and crystalize that awareness. Efficiency people, by the nature of their objectivity, not only test the effectiveness of work flow, but also test the administrative strengths and weaknesses of the top management, including the president.

Any leader who really *wants* to know where he stands in his own company can find out. Simon calls it a "lot of bunk anyway," but maybe that's a screen to cover for his own sense of "awareness."

Awareness could also cause Simon to evaluate the spiritual track he has set. It doesn't take too much probing or examining to detect whether the "spiritual atmosphere" is positive or negative. Coffee break conversation is a fairly good measure of it. Simple exchanges within that neutral atmosphere can bring out the true position the rank and file have taken with regard to the authoritarian principle. Christian workers, caught in the impracticalities and stultification of the forced spiritual overlay, become caustic, even cynical, with regard to it.

That is a basic danger point, not only for the company, but for the community outside. For if *Simon's Signposts* is producing warped personalities in terms of both the spiritual and organizational well being, can spiritual bumper stickers really be any kind of proper rationale for that? If the Christian worker looks upon his own organization with apology, or if he sees it only as a "job," then what is he going to be worth to the community where he lives? If he feels strangled by the regimented spiritual exercises, or if he goes home every night exhausted by the conflicts of trying to reconcile the dual dimensions of ministry-business, what does he really contribute to the community?

Awareness does not change things. What it does is measure "ourselves as others see us." It is, then, a primary test. And that test is the measure of God's judgment or approbation. Refusal to become aware is to create the conditions for the final slide into destruction. Awareness either confirms the rightness of the course or negates it. Awareness either shouts approval or damns. On it hangs the whole possibility of change.

Simon's refusal to become aware — or if he did, perhaps his fear to imbibe it, lest it demand change — was to bring him to the brink of ruin.

2. ANALYSIS. Awareness does not change things. It is the vestibule for change. Once aware of the pulse beat of his own rank and file, the successful Christian leader takes it for analysis, *self-analysis*. He can do that alone, or he can hire the experts to do it for him. It is a difficult part of the process or journey to change. A spiritually self-centered authoritarian, if he condescends to see any credence in becoming aware, struggles with the Gethsemane experience of self-analysis.

For one thing, analysis demands objectivity. It says, "You have heard and sensed the beat of this your kingdom. How do you see it now as a detached observer, putting yourself back to back to the facts?"

Analysis forces an inward look from the outer perspective. It forces an evaluation, a critical evaluation of self, not as some kind of "spiritual giant," but on the criteria others have used to measure him as a "Christian corporation president."

Alexander Simon's struggle is whether to go that far at all. He could charge whatever he had become aware of as "irrelevant to the larger picture." The successful Christian leader, however, sees no "larger picture" unless the component parts of that picture, all of them — their souls, feelings, sensitivities, motivations, longings — are moving with him, in concert with his aims, linked with his vision, clearly committed to the Cause as he has taken time to articulate it. Not all of them will fully grasp the meaning of the entire vision, but they will climb on to the areas open to them.

The successful Christian leader finds self-analysis, against the backdrop of the rank and file, a "brutally taxing and humbling experience." But that is the design for the shaping and reshaping of great leadership in Christian work. It sifts out the dross from the "perfect image" and says, "Simon, Simon, this is what I have against thee...."

Analysis, then, does not lead the company leader to see the corporation from where he is, but to see it from where others are. It is not an analysis in terms of balance sheets, sales figures, or profit lines, for these are not the final "success" measurements in Christian work. Rather, it is the analysis of himself in terms of the awareness of the real product — the human element — and their possession or lack of possession of goals, purpose, values, sense of belonging, involvement, personal accomplishment, etc.

But if awareness is the vestibule for change and analysis is the front room for the action, there is yet one great hurdle before anything really happens to alter the course of the organization to any degree.

3. APPLICATION. To know what's wrong, to even know that it stems from himself, means nothing to Simon and to the rank and file unless the facts are followed through to the alteration.

This is even more difficult for the "God figure." Having already presumed his own cause as "right," having concluded that "right or wrong, this is the plan of God," to have to make changes in his own leadership profile is a matter of acute stress.

But to know good and not do it, as the Scriptures warn, is the worst of sins, and it applies as much to the "founder, leader, designer, and energizer of the ark of God" as to anyone else — perhaps more so.

In the Christian organization, the leader is not privileged to hold distinctive qualities of behavior unlike his own rank and file. His own people rise only as high as the level he has set for himself. In that sense, Simon cannot afford to be a man apart. If he will not take the necessary leadership to change what everyone knows is a bad situation, then he breeds the same attitudes in his subordinates. The secular business does not run on the same sense of responsibility, because the totality of their fulfillment to rank and file is pay and position. The Christian expects more.

If awareness and analysis beg the point, then there must be *application* to effect change.

That application must begin for the "God figure" with genuine repentance before God. God is waiting too, and He is the key to what happens afterward. But this is not the kind of repentance that says, "Lord, I've been wrong ... sorry. Now if You will pick up the pieces, patch up the holes, and get it running right, I'll thank You."

No. True repentance says, "Lord, I've been wrong, and now I must make it right. *Show me how.*"

The first step in the "how" is to carry that repentance from the private closet with God to the arena where it must be diffused. He can begin with his own executive staff. This need not be a maudlin, confessional kind of thing at all. He can simply call them in, lay out new possibilities of change, and ask them to share in it with him. Allowing them to effect some of the changes is the first step in bringing an entirely new aura of responsibility and fulfillment in an area that will, in turn, move it all down the line. It may mean an admission of short-sightedness, a need to get a new sense of order into the business, and a desire to bring the entire rank and file closer together. Promise and reality must be hand in glove, however. Once it is done, even in that simple overture, the word gets out fast.

Simon need not fear that his own people are going to turn on him for his "act of contrition" or his attempt to put things right in the name of God. All authoritarian types fear this the most, as if they will lose control by the act. Yet, his own people will be quick to rise with him in his humanity, his admitted sense of frailty, his honest desire to bring them to the fullest experience in the organization. Christian work is peculiar in this one dimension. Instead of losing respect for a leader in his admission of failure, it works the other way, simply because it is what is expected in a God-centered community.

From there, the application will mean a search for other resources to build the broken fences of his own shattered business acumen. Resources for leadership are ever available. Leadership can be learned; it is not always only that which is innate. Any man thrust into such a role can make up for his lack by exposing himself to learning situations. Many a business executive well along in his years of leadership has taken the night school route to bring his own self-development up to snuff.

Everything is not going to happen all at once at *Simon's Signposts* if Simon should take the time to evaluate honestly and to make some changes. The rebuilding along specified lines will come slowly. There won't be a sudden 180 degree swing on all levels because the president is taking a "second look at things."

The matters of goals, values, purpose, jobs, status, and sense of belonging cannot all come with one stroke.

But if Simon does honestly become aware, does make his analysis and then seek to apply it where he can, there is now an *atmosphere that is conducive to change*. Once that becomes evident, the blocks to the necessary changes in other areas are torn down, and often the executives and rank and file will effect a great deal of the rest of it on their own.

There will be no trumpets blaring, no flourishes, no sudden burst of song. The rebuilding will be a piece by piece operation, at best. The old brick will come out hard. Alterations in policy and practice will tend to disrupt, put the timing off — if there was any to begin with — cause some imbalances in human relationships already somewhat molded by the "God figure."

And it won't turn into the millennium either. There will be tensions, clashes, disgruntlements. But now the atmosphere is such that it can absorb that behavior and minimize its destructive element.

But again, something will have happened. One successful Christian leader, recalling his own struggle to bring his organization to the peak of the ideal as he saw it, put it this way: "It took months to see anything different, but one day it suddenly struck home to me and to my executive assistants. There was a new wind blowing. You can't point to anybody or any one thing. You just know and sense something has happened. And you know that it is good, very good. And at that moment you just want to thank God that He waited so long, that He gave that extra shot of courage to face up to things as they were and do something about it. It's like you've been waiting for a rose to blossom and you suddenly realize that you've put it in the wrong kind of soil, given it the wrong kind of food and care. So you change it, because that rose does mean more to you than anything else right then. Then you see it start to come out, slowly, and then finally open to full beauty. You can't explain why or how that simple application could make that kind of change. Well, this company is not in full bloom yet. But it's coming. I don't think I did much to change it, and yet what I did was obviously the one thing needed to make it go, and God was pleased to help with the rest of it. It's just a beginning, but at least we are now on track."

Simon, then, can view all of this in one of two ways: he can choose to ignore the need for change and let matters remain as they are. Somehow the company will continue to function and produce and maybe even stay alive. In that case, he is willing to stay on his plateau and eventually stagnate there with what he has. The question for him is whether he has reached his highest fulfillment possible as a leader — for himself and for the people entrusted to him by God.

Or he can recognize that there are no final plateaus in God's work. It is all mountain climbing. Each level of the climb brings new experiences, new fulfillments, new dimensions of spiritual realization.

Will these simple rules of success spoil Alexander Simon? Of course not! They will "spoil" his "God figure" some. They will "spoil" a great deal of the heavy-handed leadership that smothers individual enterprise. But they won't "spoil" the treasure that he has not yet considered to be his trust.

Can *Simon's Signposts to Glory Incorporated* rise from that valley of dry bones and live? Can Alexander Simon, so molded and set in his life style credo, rise to those simple success principles? Can a complex spiritual leader ever really change?

No one can answer for Simon. But there are enough "changed ones" around to prove that it can be done.

And there really is no final shape to any man — certainly not in the Body of Christ. If there is truly experience "from glory to glory," then there is surely even more in the "darkness to light."

Maybe there is hope for Simon, as God would have him know, even in the words of the late Robert F. Kennedy:

"Few are willing to brave the disapproval of their fellows, the censure of their colleagues, the wrath of their society. Moral courage is a rarer commodity than bravery in battle or great intelligence. Yet it is the one essential, vital quality for those who seek to change a world that yields most painfully to change. And I believe that in this generation those with the courage to enter the moral conflict will find themselves with companions in every corner of the globe."

This is what Jesus must have had in mind when He faced that confused little band of twelve men who had seen all the adoring crowds disappear after Jesus had put out the terms of discipleship to them.

To His own, then, He put the simple question, "Will you also go away?" (John 6:67).

They answered the question in the only way they knew how, and at that moment laid the foundation for the greatest change ever to hit the world.

Alexander Simon has that option.

The Prayer of the Nine-to-Five Warrior

Lord, You did not promise that it would all come out to exact dimension for me in this Your vineyard. I look upon my world of tangled threads, some I know I have spun in clumsy fumbling, preoccupied with only myself and what's in it all for me; others, You know, are the work of stabbing fingers poking with careless, brazen, insensitive demand, forcing some new rip in the already torn matrix of this my Holy calling!

HOLY CALLING? I could wish for more! I look upon balance sheets, production charts, sales graphs. What poor evidence of daily effort that must make up your Kingdom in the end? I could wish for more honorable, recognized, accepted symbols of my dedication! And yet it is not the wish that counts. You know I am prone to bolt, to run! Yes, to leave it all! And yet You stand within this shambles, assuring me that this is where I must be to bring some figment of light or life, whichever You may want.

So then I could die for less, if it is Your will then, not that which man has chosen for me.

Now for him whose shadow hangs long across this tangled scene, my leader. I could wish for better things for him too that I might find it easier perhaps. But now I sense he must have his hour of second thoughts, if maybe this is not the best of all possible worlds for him as well. So maybe now we touch each other in our concerns in You — so I ask only that You give him consciousness of his own frailty that he might be conscious of mine. And in the asking, Lord, I vow to stand with him as You do, for the *product* yes, of course, which declares Your name — but more so, for the eternal hope that comes close to possibility each day, that he may rise yet to know my name, speak my name and thus, O God, to make me feel he needs me!

The Prayer of the Leader

Lord, I have come so long a journey from so small a beginning! I measure now all those steps I took in shaky faith, from scaffold to finished mortar. I remember the skinned knuckles, the torn knees, the battered senses, the long midnight hours. All to build, Lord, to build the temple in Your name, to proclaim the majesty and power of it through that which began as so simple and so mundane a conceivable idea.

So now it stands! All these years? I hold it close, Lord, as You know, guard it well, as something precious to me. I have manned its gates, walked its walls, worried every part of it to stand pure and forever durable against every storm! You know that, Lord. And You walked with me those many miles and watched with me those endless hours... and the storm has not torn one tile from its place!

And yet, Lord, there is not yet rejoicing in the camp. I feel nor sense no exuberance from these within. I make my celebration then in lonely splendor? Can this be all for all of this? Have I commanded so well the battlements and yet had not one hour to sit with these around their lonely watch-fires? The wars we fought! The wounds we took! But was it "we" then, Lord? Or was it finally that I alone presumed the battle and took the prize while these shared no sense of having fought and won?

Forgive me, Lord! My pride has frozen my heart to clay. It is hard for me to sense the necessary part they play in this final triumph. Nay, Lord, they ride with me! Now! They are not my slaves to rain flowers in my path! Help me now to bring them up, Lord, into this chariot of mine, to see the splendor You are yet to make from *our* common sweat and fearful hours, and may we never ride again our separate courses or plot our separate peace! I rise now, Lord, to embrace them in armor put aside!